A Daughter's Rhyme for The Father's Reason

**By
Anjeanette Alexander**

A Daughter's Rhyme for The Father's Reason
Copyright 2019 © by Anjeanette Alexander
ISBN: 978-0-9980262-7-5

All rights reserved. No portion of this book may be reproduced, stored in a retrieval system, or transmitted in any form or by any means—electronic, mechanical, photocopy, recording, scanning, or other—except for brief quotations in critical reviews or articles, without the prior written permission of the author.

Unless otherwise noted, Scripture quotations unmarked are taken from the KING JAMES VERSION (KJV): KING JAMES VERSION, public domain.

Scripture quotations marked (AMP) are taken from the Amplified Bible, Copyright © 1954, 1958, 1962, 1964, 1965, 1987 by The Lockman Foundation. Used by permission.

Unless otherwise indicated, all Scripture quotations are taken from THE MESSAGE, copyright © 1993, 2002, 2018 by Eugene H. Peterson. Used by permission of NavPress. All rights reserved. Represented by Tyndale House Publishers, a Division of Tyndale House Ministries.

Scripture quotations marked (NIV) are taken from the Holy Bible, New International Version®, NIV®. Copyright © 1973, 1978, 1984, 2011 by Biblica, Inc.™ Used by permission of Zondervan. All rights reserved worldwide. www.zondervan.com The "NIV" and "New International Version" are trademarks registered in the United States Patent and Trademark Office by Biblica, Inc.™

Scripture quotations marked (NLT) are taken from the Holy Bible, New Living Translation, copyright ©1996, 2004, 2015 by Tyndale House Foundation. Used by permission of Tyndale House Publishers, a Division of Tyndale House Ministries, Carol Stream, Illinois 60188. All rights reserved.

Scripture quotations marked TPT are from The Passion Translation®. Copyright © 2017, 2018 by Passion & Fire Ministries, Inc. Used by permission. All rights reserved. ThePassionTranslation.com.

In addition to the Bible, the following sources have been used in any discussion of Hebrew or Greek meanings of words, dictionary definitions, or meanings of Biblical names: Merriam-Webster.com, Blue Letter Bible.org, BibleStudyTools.com, BibleHub.com, and BibleTools.org.

Contact the author via email: aalexander@scriballyhis.com.

To my daughter, Kamaryn, the women at Gateway,
and Sister Joann

God made my life complete
when I placed all the pieces
before him.
When I got my act together,
he gave me a fresh start.
Now I'm alert to God's ways;
I don't take God for granted.
Every day I review the ways he works;
I try not to miss a trick.
I feel put back together,
and I'm watching my step.
God rewrote the text of my life
when I opened the book
of my heart to his eyes.

Psalm 18:20-24 *(THE MESSAGE)*

Table of Contents

Introduction i

Part 1: A Daughter's Rhyme

Hagar's View of Brokenness

Identity Crisis 3
The God Who Sees Me 6
Beauty for Abandoned Ashes 9

Tamar's View of Brokenness

What's in a Name? 14
The Family Business 16
Shake Off the Chains 18

My View of Brokenness

Flatline to Lifeline 21
Hitting Rock Bottom 23
Pillow Talk 24
My Time, My Temple, His Mission 25
The Black Hole of Unforgiveness 27
Crossword Love 29
The Voice 31
Fall Out Sister 33
Breaking Free 35

Part 2: The Father's Reason

Abba's View of Brokenness – The Father's Love Letters

Time to Cease and Desist 40
Where You Are 44
The Power of a Question 48

A Famine of My Word 53
A Divine Change of Clothes 56
The Purpose for the Valley 59
The Process of Bearing Fruit 62
The Secret Place 64
Time to Transition 69
For a Time Such as This 74
Mastering the Art of the Shift 78
Coming Out From Among Them 82
The Strange Woman of Fear 84
The Source of Your Life 88
The Right Position 91
The Right Posture 94
The Misconception of Time 97
Timelessness Inside of You 100
A Steward of My Word 103
This Kind of Longsuffering 106
This Kind of Sacrifice 111
This Kind of Love 114
This Kind of Covenant 117
Exposing the Enemy's Roots 120
Reviving Your Soul 125
Picking Up Your Tools of Warfare 128

Appendix 135

Acknowledgements 147

INTRODUCTION

Conversations between Broken Vessels
and the Potter

Satisfy me in your sweetness,
and my song of joy will return.
The places within me
you have crushed
will rejoice in
your healing touch.
Psalm 51:8 (TPT)

The sacrifices of God
are a broken spirit: a broken
and a contrite heart,
O God, thou wilt not despise.
Psalm 51:17

When we find ourselves in a season of brokenness, what is *our response*?

When we enter a season of warfare, what do we do? When we discover that it is our time to mourn, give up, weep, or tear down (Ecclesiastes 3:1-8), to whom do we run? When we realize it is our time to scatter, refrain, throw away, or be silent, will we do it? When we understand that the season for someone or something has ended, will we let go?

God has allowed us to enter this broken place for a reason, what will be our response?

We have different ways of coping with our circumstances. Some of us may withdraw and seek solitude, write poetry, or capture our thoughts in journals. We may draw or paint, pray and meditate on scriptures, or take long walks. Some of us may write little notes to God in the margins of our bibles or address letters to Him in notebooks. Whatever we do to cope, we long to hear His response and feel His love through our trials.

For many of us, we want to know why. We seek the lesson behind the brokenness and attempt to make sense of it all, but let's be honest. Sometimes our seasons of brokenness have no rhyme or reason to them. They really *hit* us hard. Our response time lags because we do not know what to do. Our broken place is where we live out the words of that old hymn and request to "have a little talk with Jesus."

We just know that we need someone who is powerful enough to put our broken pieces together and help us to move forward. It is a delicate time of transparency where we should be mentally, emotionally, and spiritually naked and unashamed before God. We lay our inward parts (mind, emotions, and will) in front of Him, not for condemnation and judgment, but for truth, wisdom, and purification (Psalm 51:6; Proverbs 20:27; Proverbs 20:30; Jeremiah 31:33).

It is a time of testing in which God expects us to apply what we have learned in the scriptures to what we are going through. If we have neglected our relationship with Him or never had one at all, it is a time of introduction and rededication. We must examine our brokenness through spiritual discernment, and our response must be one of humility. We should ask ourselves if our disobedience or choices have led us to this broken place like David did Psalm 51. For some of us, this season of brokenness calls for a time of vulnerability and submission in which we stop running from God and run back to Him.

> Now Jesus was in Bethany, in the home of Simon, a man Jesus had healed of leprosy. And as he was reclining at the table, a woman came into the house, holding an alabaster flask. It was filled with the highest quality of fragrant and expensive oil. *She walked right up to Jesus, and with a gesture of extreme devotion,* she broke the flask and poured out the precious oil over his head.
> **Mark 14:3 (TPT)**

Vessels are delicate containers made of precious material. Painted with beautiful, ornate designs, they may contain plants, oil, water, or fragrances. Their contents are valuable and necessary. When a vessel breaks, it leaves a big mess. Depending on how shattered it is, the container can be restored with strong, adhesive glue.

Some of us may discard or reject it because the brokenness has altered the vessel's beauty and usefulness. We may question why we should put all this energy into restoring it. If we allow the deep to call us to a deeper enlightenment of our spiritual eyes, we see the beauty in the broken pieces. They speak of a testimony of survival and victory that still makes the vessel of use. What better example of this testimony than the one of our Savior? Jesus was the stone that the builders rejected, but now He is the chief cornerstone (Psalm 118:22 AMP).

In Isaiah 61:3, we learn that there is beauty for our ashes and the oil of joy for our mourning. For the oil to flow or the ashes to become beautiful, we must be broken. In 2

Corinthians 4:7, Paul tells the believers at Corinth that we have treasure in earthen vessels. This treasure, the gift of the Holy Spirit, shows the greatness of God in us and through us. When we are weak, He is our strength. Where we are broken, He flows through us and makes us complete in Him. *Our brokenness draws us to a higher level in our relationship with God.*

In addition to the value, beauty, and usefulness of broken vessels, we tend to underestimate the amount of the precious material that is in them. We have been shattered by a storm like Paul, each of us hanging on to our own little piece (Acts 27:44) and thinking that we are left with little to nothing even though we still have *a piece*. If we perceive a lack of adequate supply, we immediately evaluate *our* sources. We conclude that they are insufficient in producing the resources we need, but our focus is misdirected. God is the Source. He took a dark and void earth, formed and filled it with His creative mind, and set mankind in the Garden of Eden where abundance flowed. God is a God of the overflow, our El Shaddai (Genesis 17:1). He works wonders with small numbers; that's the key to divine multiplication.

Remember the mustard seed is the smallest of its kind, but it yields a tree so large that birds can find a haven (Mark 4:30-32). It follows the pattern of the kingdom of heaven. The little boy had five fish and two loaves of bread, but it fed 5,000 people. He uses us as broken people of small stature and sinful nature to carry out dreams and visions that seem beyond our reach.

In 1 Kings 17 and 2 Kings 4, two widows with vessels had the same mindset about the few resources they possessed. Each woman judged the sufficiency of what they had through the lens of lack, but the men of God, Elijah and Elisha, saw the potential through the lens of faith. The widow of Zarephath had a cruse of oil and a little flour that never ran out as she made cakes for her son and Elijah. The second widow's oil filled every vessel in her house, and she sold the oil to pay off her debtors just like Elisha prophesied. When faith is the substance of things hoped for and the evidence of things not seen (Hebrews 11:1), *broken vessels showcase the power, dominion, and glory of God.*

Broken vessels known by their past reputation may feel like their quality has been diminished because of their fall. If they are in an art gallery, a nursery, or someone's home, people who are familiar with their former state may deem them unworthy to be a part of their collection. In John 4, the woman at the well had a reputation for being with many men. She went about her day as usual as she prepared to get water from the well. She didn't know that Jesus had made a special stop in Samaria just for her because he had a prodigal daughter that He needed to bring home. As she and Jesus talked and the woman revealed what everyone else defined as worship, He explained to her that true worship was in spirit and in truth.

The woman at the well received the divine revelation that anyone could have a relationship with God despite past or current situations. She had been married several times and currently lived unmarried with a man. However, Jesus, the Son of God, put aside his traveling itinerary to give her the choice to be in right relationship with Him. The woman probably realized that not only natural water, but also natural man could not quench her spiritual thirst. Her brokenness produced leaks within her spiritual vessel, but this manner of man who asked for a cup of water provided her needs, healed her broken places, and affirmed her worthiness.

The woman at the well dropped her water pot and evangelized the same men who labeled her by her brokenness. Worship is when a broken vessel, immersed in the miry clay of life, has the grace to come into the Lord's presence. In His presence, the broken vessel can be transparent while giving reverence to God. While worshipping, it can be made whole so that the broken vessel can carry out its divine purpose (Isaiah 6:1-8). *Broken vessels still have purpose in the Kingdom.*

In Luke's version of the woman with the alabaster box (Luke 7:36-50), her brokenness was her identity. As a broken vessel, she entered Simon the Pharisee's house. The woman wept in godly sorrow while carrying an alabaster jar of expensive, fragrant oil. She poured it on top of Jesus' head and used her tears to wipe His feet with her hair.

One of the disciples, whom many scholars believed to be Judas, became offended because the oil could have been sold instead of wasted. Simon the Pharisee's offense came from his judgment of her sinful life. He wondered why Jesus would let someone broken by sin touch Him. To the Pharisee, her sin disqualified her to be in the presence of anything godly. Through a parable on forgiveness, Jesus taught him otherwise. He told Simon and the other spectators in the house that the woman showed more honor and reverence than any of them because of her humility. Because of her contrite heart and broken spirit, Jesus forgave her sins. *Broken vessels are an altar that releases the sweet fragrance of worship to God.*

> I will give you back your health
> and heal your wounds," says the Lord.
> "For you are called an outcast—
> 'Jerusalem for whom no one cares.'"
> This is what the Lord says:
> "When I bring Israel home again from captivity
> and restore their fortunes,
> Jerusalem will be rebuilt on its ruins,
> and the palace reconstructed as before.
> **Jeremiah 30:17-18 (NLT)**

> Distress that drives us to God [godly sorrow] does that. It turns us around. It gets us back in the way of salvation. We never regret that kind of pain. But those who let distress drive them away from God [worldly sorrow] are full of regrets, end up on a deathbed of regrets. And now, isn't it wonderful all the ways in which this distress has goaded [brought] you closer to God? You're more alive, more concerned, more sensitive, more reverent, more human, more passionate, more responsible. Looked at from any angle, you've come out of this with *purity of heart (emphasis added)*.
> **2 Corinthians 7:10-11 (THE MESSAGE)**

The people had been scattered from their homeland for seventy-two years. In the middle of their brokenness, they had grown accustomed to their place of exile. The people had families, land, and prosperity as they lived under the rule of the kings of Babylon and Persia. Before exile, the people were one country, but division split their national identity into two regions: Israel and Judah. Each nation separated themselves from each other and God.

Assyria conquered Israel 1st, and then Babylon led three strategic raids that destroyed the walls of Jerusalem and brought the Israelites of Judah into exile. The Lord prophesied through His prophets that Jerusalem would be rebuilt and restored, but many years of being in the same broken place caused some Israelites to become comfortable where they were.

King Cyrus of Persia defeated the Babylonians and gained control of the land. God declared in Isaiah 45 that He would make the crooked places straight and use King Cyrus as a part of His plan of restoration after the exile. Ezra enters the scene as a scribe and a priest. He, along with the prophets Haggai and Zechariah and the cupbearer/visionary Nehemiah, coordinated the effort to rebuild Jerusalem's walls, gates, and the temple. The power of the writer's inkhorn as a tool could be seen in Ezra's hands. He used the power of the written word and intercession to bring about a spiritual revival among the Israelites. In their season of brokenness, they lost hope and became discouraged. However, a word spoken in good season reminded them of how they got there, who God was, and why it was important to restore their covenant with Him.

The books of Ezra and Nehemiah are important reads for us when we are trying to rebuild and restore our lives after a season of brokenness. In each book, the enemy operated through many people who adamantly opposed and scoffed at the Israelites. These enemies wanted the people's dysfunction or their stuck place to be a permanent residence when God only intended it to be a temporary location.

By the leading of the Holy Spirit, Ezra and Nehemiah knew that God had the Israelites in a process. With prayer, worship, consecration, and prophetic declarations of God's word, the men kept the focus of Israel on *going through* the process instead of *remaining* in it.

A process was designed to take them through a series of stages that result in a true spiritual transformation. If they had listened to the distractions of the enemy or focused on where they were, the Israelites could have risked the opportunity for a process to turn into a cycle. They had to transition effectively from brokenness to restoration, but the Israelites needed their spiritual father to guide them with the wisdom of His word.

>Behold, the LORD hath proclaimed
>unto the end of the world,
>Say ye to the daughter of Zion,

> Behold, thy salvation cometh;
> behold, his reward *is* with him,
> and his work before him.
> **Isaiah 62:11**

Just like our natural parents guide us as we grow from infants to young adults, our Heavenly Father leads us as through the stages of our spiritual walk with Him. We need Abba Father (Mark 14:36; Romans 8:15; Galatians 4:6) to help us transition through the many seasons that take us from our broken place to our spiritually wealthy place in faith, hope, and love in Him.

The Lord affectionately calls each of us, Daughter of Zion. In the Bible, He used it as a compassionate name to refer to the nation of Israel. He also called them a bride unto Him and His sheep. These metaphors are only expressions of the covenant love, grace, and mercy that the Lord has for us. When we are in our broken places, we do have times when we feel like we can't trace God or feel His presence and love. We must understand that He is allowing this brokenness to strengthen our faith and trust in Him and to come to a deeper revelation of who He is.

> Put me in remembrance:
> let us plead together:
> declare thou, that
> thou mayest be justified.
> **Isaiah 43:26**

A Daughter's Rhyme for The Father's Reason is a conversation about brokenness between a daughter and Abba Father. The first section, "A Daughter's Rhyme," is her view of brokenness from start to finish. She writes in poems to the Lord as she tries to understand her process.

Poems are an art form whose stanzas capture imagery, intimacy, and transparency. They are literary spaces that uncover the beautiful meaning behind the human experience.

Poetry is the platform that Hagar and Tamar, two Biblical daughters, share their stories of brokenness. Scriptural references are provided to give the complete details of their stories. The last section is my view of brokenness told in poetry. My scriptural references are some of the verses that God gave me through my process to anchor my soul in my broken place. Each daughter—Hagar, Tamar, & I—has a verse that captures the central message of each section of poetry.

The second section, "The Father's Reason," is God's response to His daughters. He explains the purpose of their brokenness and the lessons He wants them to learn. More importantly, He shares His love and conveys His desire for them to become the kingdom daughters He has always wanted them to be.

The appendix has Abba Father's final words to His daughters and my prayer for them, along with two strategies to help you navigate seasons of brokenness. My sincere hope is that this book will meet you at your point of need as you hear God's voice and experience His love. May God bless you, dear Daughter of Zion!

Part 1: A Daughter's Rhyme

We have become his poetry,
a re-created people
that will fulfill the destiny
he has given each of us,
for we are joined to Jesus,
the Anointed One.
Even before we were born,
God planned in advance
our destiny and the good works
we would do to fulfill it!
Ephesians 2:10 (TPT)

Hagar's View of Brokenness

Genesis 12:14-20
Genesis 16:1-16
Genesis 21:8-21
Galatians 4:22-31

If your heart is broken,
you'll find God right there;
if you're kicked in the gut,
he'll help you catch your breath.
Psalm 34:18 (THE MESSAGE)

Identity Crisis

Am I *still* Hagar?

I
       am
              broken. . .

a stranger in *this*
land, a lost one from Egypt,
faith being tested.

many gods i serve,
Pharaoh standing among them,
self-idolatry.

Nile River, its flow
deeply running through my veins,
my heart lifted high.

my pride on trial,
as a part of Pharaoh's trade,
given to Abram

for the precious hand
of Hebrew princess, Sarai.
betrothed not a sister,

but a wife. Abram's
lie that sets off plagues
upon Pharaoh's house.

no even exchange
just her release, a relief
from his affliction.

i am a stranger in this land—

Sarai's handmaid, prone
to all her demands, no say
in recent request.

citizen, servant,
now concubine, her plan
to birth a promise.

what you nowadays
politically correct
as another wife

or surrogate mom.
not sure if the plan would work,
a better status

if i can succeed.
night after night we try,
child now soon to come.

pride like a lion,
with contempt for my mistress,
my success i flaunt.

i am a stranger in this land—

Sarai's barren womb
and old age, always first wife,
never a mom like me,

assuming I have
given an answer to God's
prophetic decree.

Abram's heart and mine
joined as one, my lovelorn eyes
drawing Sarai's scorn.

mistreated so much,
asking idols, even God,
why my fertile womb

that succeeded in
giving Abram a son now
makes me feel less than.

bruise after bruise, her
harsh rebukes hitting targets—
my ego downsized.

i am a stranger in this land—

heart and pride broken,
no longer know who I am
my life forever

trapped in fragments,
syllables, lines—a love poem
becoming undone.

to Egypt, my home
wind erasing my footprints,
tears in desert sun.

i am now a stranger in this body—

running

      from

           this

                 land.

The God Who Sees Me

I'm living out the meaning of my name.
I'm in flight through the wilderness.
No water in sight, my soul thirsts.

Sweat drips in my eyes. Salty rivulets
form tributaries of transparency,
along with my tears.

Weariness jolts through my bones
and pierces the marrow. A weight
of loneliness settles like sediments
of sorrow. It feels like gravel
deep down in my soul.

My knees buckle as I fall
to the sandy ground. My pride
is my dysfunction, a wayward
compass. Direction nowhere to be
found, its needle spins beside me.

We go in circles, the needle and I,
a cycle that is now being broken.
The violence of emptying myself

of the I that dwells inside
covers my soul like a garment,
a separation akin to the cutting
away of dead skin.

I cry out to my gods. *No response.*
Wondering as I wander if I have
angered them. Idols with eyes
of no sight and ears of no sound.

Hagar, Hagar. . .

A still, small voice—
or maybe it is just the wind.
Heat exhaustion begets delirium.

Hagar, Hagar, Sarai's maidservant...

I'm too weak to lift my head or raise my voice.
Just enough despair and hopelessness
to curse my regretted choice.

From where did you come?

Is this the God of Abram that I hear?
Far, far away from Egypt, and now free
from my mistress, Sarai.

Where are you?

Can't You see me?
I am trapped between hard-pressed sand
and a cloudless sky with an endless horizon,
a height I will never be able to reach.

What are you doing here?

Do You not know? Do You not care?
I am stuck between a place called *theirs*,
their land, *their* promise, *their* God
and a place called *here* where my idols
covet hard for the faint beat of my heart.

Where are you going?

Honestly, Lord, I don't know. Headed toward
my native land to heal from the hurt of a man
allowing his wife to have her way with me.
Now I wallow in self-pity, resigning to stay where I am.
I feel like a curse that's been chosen to birth a promise.
Have you come to finish what she started?

*I have heard your affliction, and I have answered you.
Ishmael shall also become a nation, but no child
of promise will he be. I promise to provide for you two.
Don't you hear the fountain flowing behind you?*

Yes, my Lord, I can see it in clear view.
It's also bubbling forth inside of me.
I am a broken vessel who has now become whole.
I sought salvation from an idol, but I didn't find it
until I drank from Your well.

*Humble yourself and return to your mistress.
Give birth to your son, Ishmael, for he shall live.
His fighting spirit will follow him, but neither
he nor you will suffer. Go back and watch
the yet-to-be told story unfold.*

Strength stirs within my settled soul.
The God Who Sees, El Roi, has run
after the wayward girl on the run.

The God Who Sees loves me more
than any man or god ever could. Joy
is now a spring flowing inside my soul.

I now honor Him with my prayers,
dedicating this spring to Him,
along with my heart.

Beauty for Abandoned Ashes

There shall be beauty for your abandoned ashes.

Ishmael has grown over the years.
His cherubic face and plump body
now stretches out into a lanky adolescent.

My face beams with love as I witness
God's living example of answering my call
and dealing with my affliction.
He is a God of His word.

I see the change in Abram and my mistress, Sarai.
His Spirit transformed them in front of my eyes.
Abram became Abraham; Sarai became Sarah.
Ishmael and I remain the same.

Our names never changed, but our position
in God did. Abraham's God invited every male—
Hebrew and foreigner in his camp
to enter a covenant with Him.

There shall be beauty for your abandoned ashes.

I humbled myself unto my mistress.
Each day becomes easier and easier.
At first a drop of compassion struggles
to flow from Sarai's hardened heart.

Then a steady stream
of tolerance fills the gap
between us—bondwoman
and the woman born free.

A child born out of affliction—
a gain of a son, a loss of self,
the seed of the law of time,
the fruit of the flesh.

A child born out of faith—
the invisible, now visible;
the word of God, now
tangible evidence, a gain
of an heir, a loss of infertility,
the seed of grace manifesting
through timelessness,
the fruit of God's Spirit.
Two different seeds,
two nations inside sons,
covered by one covenant,
blessed by different inheritances.

My wilderness experience
became my classroom,
learning to think of her more
and me less, submitting
to the one over me as I now
know what it means to do
all work unto the Lord.

There shall be beauty for your abandoned ashes.

The birth of Isaac, the gift of laughter,
the manifestation of God's promise,
now resounds through the camp.
Ishmael's little brother is finally here.
God is a God of His word.

With the time to laugh comes
the time to weep. With the time
of welcoming a new son comes
the rejecting of the other.

Ishmael mocked his little brother.
Contempt entered Sarah's heart.
Now my name is no longer Hagar.
She belittles me to a nameless label
that spews from her mouth:
"Cast out the *bondwoman!*"

Cast out the reminder
of Sarai's mistake. Cast out
the firstborn who can
receive no blessing
or inheritance in her eyes.

Cast out the woman and her son
whom Abram affectionately
cares for and intercedes for
to God daily.

With a little bread, a little water,
his eyes averted and heart downcast,
Abram heeds God's word and sends us
away. I don't understand. It doesn't
make sense. I also yielded to *God's word*.

Humbled and submitted to Sarah,
I trusted His word that Ishmael would
grow into a young man and a father of
a nation. He promised him a place
through His covenant of circumcision.

At God's word,
our lives crumble to ashes,
as we enter the heat of the desert,
a land and life of the unknown,
completely abandoned.

There shall be beauty for your abandoned ashes.

Abandonment is like being attached
to a dead root that I cannot sever.
The connection to what once
lived—the relationship, the family,
the stability, and the love—have ended.

Another woman and son have taken
our place. The cut—sudden and jarring—
no time to prepare, no way to cope
with the huge void that now exists.

Ishmael and I have been discarded
with such disdain. As supplies decrease,
my son's cries pierce my heart. I lay him
far from me and weep tears of defeat.

There shall be beauty for your abandoned ashes.

I hear God's voice again.
He tells me to fear not.
A well of water appears.
He tells me to arise.
A promise to make Ishmael
a great nation is spoken again.

I place my son in my arms,
hold the bottle of water to his lips.
And God *is* with me and Ishmael,
in the wilderness of Paran, our new home.
God is a God of His word.

I rise from the ashes like a phoenix.
My broken pieces become the platform
that preaches a sermon of victory
over a hopeless situation.
My abandoned ashes have
become the beauty unto holiness
to the God Who Sees. There will be
glory after this.

Tamar's View of Brokenness

2 Samuel 13:1-39
2 Samuel 14:27

Wake up, wake up, O Zion!
Clothe yourself with strength.
Put on your beautiful clothes,
O holy city of Jerusalem,
for unclean and godless people
will enter your gates no longer.

Rise from the dust, O Jerusalem.
Sit in a place of honor.
Remove the chains
of slavery from your neck,
O captive daughter of Zion.
Isaiah 52:1-2 (NLT)

What's in a Name?

> When I look at you, I see
> how you have taken
> my fruit and tasted
> my word. Your life
> has become clean
> and pure, like a lamb
> washed and newly shorn.
> You now show grace
> and balance with truth
> on display.
> **Song of Solomon 4:2 (TPT)**

I am a palm tree, replete with date fruit
sweet to the soul like anointed words
of truth on a parchment scroll. My trunk
is full of stems arranged like burnished gold,
a trunk of well-built armor where thousands
of shields hang. They do not bend
or buckle in any wind-tossed storm.
I am like a tower of David.

I am a palm tree, replete with fronds
and branches that flourish. Leaves of
healing and beauty that glorify the
Creator. I am statuesque as I stand
beside wells of water and in cities
of influence like Elim and Jericho.
I am a well-watered garden, a fountain
of living water, purified and prepared
for the master's use. A set apart one
in a family of male heirs.
I am the daughter of David.

I am a palm tree, replete with royal
significance. My boughs and branches

used in worship, prophetically penned
by Ezekiel and Joel. An intricate lineage
of roots grounded in history and heritage
flows from the core of who I am.
The kingdom is at hand in my bloodline.
I am a branch in David's family tree.

I am a palm tree, replete with fertile roots
whose origin started with Judah's daughter-in-law,
a widowed wife shunned and shuffled around
as she secured a male heir, Perez, through
the ruse of a veil, a kinswoman who models
how to rise above adversity.

I am a root sprawling with offshoots of greats
and grands—Boaz, Obed, and Jesse, each one
a testament of the power of God in their lives.
A second root of nobility grafted in
through my grandfather, King Talmai,
and my mother, Maacah's father.
I am a fair maiden and an arrow
in the quiver of King David.

I am Tamar.

The Family Business

> Now, therefore, the sword
> shall never depart from your
> house, because you have
> despised Me and have taken
> the wife of Uriah the Hittite
> to be your wife. Thus says
> the Lord, 'Behold, I will
> stir up evil against you
> from your own household;
> **2 Samuel 12:10-11a (AMP)**

The thought of *it* is a stronghold,
a set of mental chain links
holding me hostage inside.

The gravity of *it*
is too much to bear.
I go back to the comfort
zone of a nursery rhyme:

Father killed his ten thousands.
Father was sought after by King Saul.
Father finally got the throne.
Then Father had a great moral fall.
Father's actions didn't affect
just one child. Father's actions

affected

us

all.

Father killed his ten thousands.
Father was sought after by King Saul.
Father finally got the throne.

Then Father had a great moral fall.
Father's actions didn't affect
just one child. Father's actions

affected

us

all.

The family business is in every mouth
and ear. The sword of lust transferred
from father to Amnon; the sword of murder
to Absalom. Absalom tried to restore
my honor, first by vengeance followed
by mutiny, then by giving his daughter
my name. I lost him to death, too.
Now I wither away into a deeper state
of mourning, grief and regret.

The stately palm tree now shattered.
I am an alabaster box of tears, shame,
and often-asked questions of why.

What once grounded
this maiden formerly known
as Tamar has been uprooted.

The thought of *it* is a stronghold,
a set of mental chain links
holding me hostage inside.

If only God will arise with compassion
and favor in His wings, then far from
this family business, I would rise.

Shake Off the Chains

> My beloved spake,
> and said unto me,
> Rise up, my love,
> my fair one,
> and come away.
> For, lo, the winter is past,
> the rain is over and gone;
> The flowers appear
> on the earth; the time
> of the singing
> of birds is come.
> **Song of Solomon 2:10-12b**

I am God's beloved, His precious daughter,
no longer a lost one drowning underwater.

I rise from sackcloth and ashes to shake off chains,
shifting from Amnon to God the control of my reins.

No longer in communion with guilt and shame,
Time alone with God has helped me reclaim my name.

Sure, the culture full of rules and traditions and such,
say I am not worthy to wed, not good for much.

Resigning to their labels, my chest that I clutch,
Absalom's home as a prison to hide, if it had not been
for a gentle touch.

Awake from my spiritual stupor, led to my father's psalms,
filled with joy and strength, He grabbed my palms.

Shackles off my feet, I dance on my broken bones,
Joy of my salvation restored, now I'm never alone.

Mourning ending, morning beginning
I am God's beloved: My heart's singing.

My View of Brokenness

Matthew 6:25-33
Romans 4:20-23
Hebrews 10:35-38
Joshua 1:2-9

My heart is stirred by a noble theme
as I recite my verses for the king;
my tongue is the pen of a skillful writer.
Psalm 45:1 (NIV)

Flatline to Lifeline

The last hit has made its mark
A flatline streaks through the monitor
Ashes almost turned into dust.

Death does not become me
I shall live and not die
With eyes lifted to the hills,
I trust. . .

My breath shall enter you and give you life

Welcome back, daughter!
I have wrapped you in the Holy Spirit
A garment of grace
holding your brokenness in place
This place is a blank canvas
Unformed, but filled with potential
Change your view
Adopt the right motive.

Here, you will bear fruit that remains

You are my burning one
An angel of my light and glory
Let my love shine through you
My voice transforms the enemy's flood
into walls of water to create a path
You are now on dry land.

He meant it for evil; I meant it for your good

My grace covers your sins and mistakes
Join me in my covenant that I will never forsake
Come to the secret place
There is healing here
Let me tend to you

Cast your cares upon me
Enter in and I will give you rest.

Worship me in the beauty of holiness, Zion

Lifeline extended
I lie prostrate before Him
Morning, noon, and night
I soak in His presence
His word is my meat and drink
My process of tried, tested, and true begins.
I'm hoping my faith does not bend.

Hitting Rock Bottom

I look like you
But on the inside
it is a different story
I'm broken into fragments
A divided, dis-united states
No constitution
Waiting for a Lamb
Worthy to break the seals
Got my hands up
Woke
SOS flags waving erratically
May day, May day
The breakers are crashing
My hopes and dreams are dashing
Straight places become crooked
Mountains collapse into valleys
I'm a pile of dry bones
No wind in sight
Falling apart
Silent cries fill my heart
I'm broken inside
Holy Spirit, save me!
He took me by the hand
and said, "It's not a matter of fact;
it's a matter of trust."

Pillow Talk

There is no soundness
from head to toe, open wounds
a beacon of fear.

Come, let us reason together.

But the door is shut.
No way of escape in sight
Spiritual scales lie.

Draw near and see men as trees walking.

This mountain won't move
Fig trees with no fruit of faith
My roots are showing.

If only you would believe.

I lay down with doubt
I pick up faith, then drop it.
You remain faithful.

I cannot reject what I have accepted.

Fear has always told me
if I fail, I disappoint you
I can't bear to lose your love.

My love covers a multitude of sins.
When will you let it come in?

My Time, My Temple, His Mission

My temple exists no more
Dismantled from top to bottom
Curtain rent in two, true altars revealed
Broken dreams and lost time
set up as the holy of holies.

He said He would tear down this temple.
I just didn't know:
The temple was me.

This time of reconstruction has extended
Three days have past
When did the blueprint change?
I thought time was of the essence.

My timeline didn't quite sync up to His
The renovation now seems irrelevant
Stationary things are being moved around
This moment of transition hurts
Left me feeling exposed
The whole world can see I'm undone.

This new altar is hard to worship
To serve you requires obedience
for the blessed to manifest
This acceptable time doesn't feel. . .
so acceptable.

I fret a little, my soul disquieted
What if the temple is completed, but
it is too late for it to be of any effect?
Arms wrap around me
A fatherly kiss He gives
Daughter, I am timeless;
therefore, I am always relevant.

Be willing and obedient
You will eat the good
of the land.

I am building this temple
to dwell inside of you
so that I can walk among them.
You are not the only one
I was sent to save and rebuild.

The Black Hole of Unforgiveness

I wonder how black holes form,
dark abysses with swirling stars—
an accurate address
of the state of my heart.

My soul's been drifting for a while,
untethered in a vast void,
growing deeper and deeper
in unforgiveness.

I've lost my true self,
forgotten wings of forgiveness;
the time has come for this to end.

For cycles of self-destruction
have become galaxies of dysfunction.

Year of promotion retained

Summer school has begun.
This black hole must be filled
with the light of love—
Pure, untainted, unconditional.

What manner of man can love like this?

Then a suddenly occurs.
Once nailed feet step
on my heart's murky waters.
He bears a cross on his shoulders.

Eyes ablaze with an eternal love,
He encourages me with these words:
"Forgive them like I forgave you."

At that moment, I die to self,
each tie broken; my soul free.
I pick up my cross, humbled.
Thanks to the Son risen
with healing in His wings.

Crossword Love

First word, five letters down
Head settled in heaven's authority,
bowed in submission to His father.
Feet crossed with spiked nails;
heels filled with dominion.

Five letters may be read down
but their impact is up—
Upward bound, restoring a godly bond,
reconnecting a lost first love.

Tis so sweet to say His name
The answer to death in my sin-stricken frame:
Jesus.

Second word, six letters across
Arms horizontally spread out
Nailed hands that once dried up
a fountain of blood with one touch,
now release living water from wells
of salvation to connect all
to the household of faith.

The color of red is the color of love
The answer that unifies us all in the world:
Christ.

Last word, eight letters across and down
A new beginning of an unwritten epistle
My tongue is the pen of a ready writer
inscribed with the law of love and kindness.

I'm in love like never before.
It's a tight-gripped hug kind of love
It's a read my bible for hours kind of love
It's an overlook that you cut me

deep kind of love.
It's a mercy-filled, it's cool they rejected,
abandoned, or talked about me
kind of love.

Many are puzzled by the change in me.
The answer to their head-scratching question:
The Cross.

The Voice

I appear before four judges
who have disappointed God
by pretending to be Him in my life.
I have allowed each one to become—
my American idol.

Each voice is a different sound:

a boisterous wind,
a rumbling quake,
a crackling fire.
the off-key soundtrack
of my mind stuck on repeat.

The backs of their chairs face me
They mock my attempt
to break through their noise.

Cry loud, spare not.
Raise your voice
like Heaven's trumpet.

In the eye of the verbal storm,
I hear His still, small voice.

Fire is suddenly shut up in my bones
The rush, the force, the power
cannot be contained.
It gushes forth from my lips,
a download from His throne.

Tributaries of His love and word
resurrect the audience's broken dreams,
along with my own.

Each chair turns around quickly,
hands frozen over their buzzers
until the Father's voice interrupts
their regularly scheduled program.

No need for them to affirm
whom He has already blessed.
I drop the mic, along with their yokes,
my voice now restored.

Fall Out Sister

Dear John letter tucked
between tear-stained pillows
A down comforter
on a bed that once confined me
It's half past the hour for me
to move from *here* to *there*.
Inside, my Comforter quickens.

"Fall out," he commands.
Out of agreement, I fall.
With new spiritual armor,
he equips me.

A changing of the guards
New general, the Lord of hosts
takes the lead role in my life.

He calls me to stand,
flat-footed and face like flint,
on blood-shed covenant promises
that salvation and deliverance
fulfilled when the Cross crossed
roads paved by mankind's sin.
"Fall in," says the Lord of hosts.

I obey him like a good soldier,
and carry out His commission.
I now approach you
and say, "Fall out, sister."

Will you heed the call
to join the ranks
of faith-filled witnesses?

You've dwelled in this mountain
long enough, time out
for hiding in the trenches.

Fall out, sister,
from the agreement
you've held with this wilderness.
You've made a sojourn
into a permanent stay.

Fall in line instead
with the Master's plan.
Rise up, take up your bed,
and walk, soldier.
Fall out, sister—
and march forward.

Breaking Free

I am now walking as one—
The enemy is long gone.
Torment, negativity,
anxiety and fear replaced
by the Savior's good cheer.
Devil's la familia tried
to make me loco.
Fighting me
with staves and lies.
Auctioning off my flesh
to the birds of the skies.

They sat in the boardroom
of Destiny Killer Central,
A charge to keep
for my soul to bind.
Three-stage battle strategy
they did devise:
Kill my hope.
Steal my identity,
Destroy my mind.
Oh, he thought
he was so wise.

One mistake
robbed him of a TKO
He let worship
from my mouth flow,
Had me on the ropes.
Bullies caving in.
Ready to record
a tally on the board
for his anticipated win.

A divine interruption
occurred to his chagrin.
The Lord heard my cry.
He rent the heavens
and lit up the sky.
His righteous right hand
grabbed mine.

"Daughter, tag me in."

He fought my battle
with all His might.
I am now settled,
truly traveling light,
many lessons learned.

Now I slay giants with the name
of the Lord of Hosts.
In His Spirit lies the chalk lines
of my spiritual foes.

Now I know
the strategy of Heaven:
Pass the battle
to the Lord through prayer.
Read His playbook
until its wear and tear.
Let Heaven touch down
and break me free.

Join the cloud of witnesses
From Abel to John the Baptist
and all in-between—
By faith, all have won the victory.
We break from the huddle.
Head bruised in enmity,
my enemy is befuddled.

Victory is won; the battle is over—
But the series does not end.
The hunger games of the broken
who yearn for righteousness,
now the Lord must win.

The inkhorn as my sword,
the book of Eli as my guide.
I write breakthrough words
on shards of ostraca
with the Holy Spirit by my side.

I am now walking as one,
looking for others to join me,
a kingdom threat to the enemy,
purposed in breaking others free.

Part 2: The Father's Reason

Come now, and let us
reason together,
saith the LORD.
Isaiah 1:18a

Trust in the Lord with all your heart;
do not depend on your own
understanding. Seek his will
in all you do, and he will show
you which path to take.
Don't be impressed with
your own wisdom. Instead, fear
the Lord and turn away from evil.
Then you will have healing
for your body and strength
for your bones.
Proverbs 3:5-8 (NLT)

Abba's View of Brokenness
The Father's Love Letters

Yet God has made everything beautiful
for its own time. He has planted
eternity in the human heart,
but even so, people cannot see
the whole scope of God's work
from beginning to end.
Ecclesiastes 3:11 (NLT)

Time to Cease and Desist

Dear Daughter of Zion,

To be broken is a difficult place to be.

It has taken you into the dark unknown where faulty foundations are shaken. You have hit rock bottom. You don't quite know how to end the cycle, but the pain is unbearable. You sit in the middle of the broken pieces in despair because you don't know how to put them together.

This broken place is a threshing floor in which you are crushed like an olive. It is a place of discomfort where I separate the tares that hinder your productivity from the beautiful wheat that I desire you to become. You are uncomfortable and restless because this broken place feels like a piece of clothing or an old wineskin that no longer fits, but you are ambivalent about letting it go (Luke 5:36-39). It is a place where heavy burdens weigh you down and wear you out. You search for a way out of it by trying to relieve the pressure and release the weight.

What broke you is not your end. Do not make it your new residence. Surely, there is an end that must come to this season of brokenness, and a future that will result in your hope and expectation being met. Just like Isaac broke through hardened soil to access fresh water in closed wells, I am using your brokenness to release a fresh outpouring of the Holy Spirit in you. I have cradled you in my hand as you have knelt on the floor with your tears as your meat. I am commanding my lovingkindness towards you in the morning and giving you a song of praise during the night.

Daughter, you are not the only one who has been in a broken place. In Mark 5:1-13, the man from Gadarenes lived in a state of brokenness. He refused to put away dead things like his mindset, his connections, or his old way of life. Instead he took up residence among the tombs and resorted to methods of escape like cutting himself with stones. He screamed constantly in a failed attempt to break the mental bands of torment. Isolated from everyone, this man carried a legion of spirits that vexed him. The Gadarenes man struggled against anyone who tried to put him in chains. Each iron fetter he broke with supernatural strength, yet the spiritual chains would not bend.

Daughter, do you know that vexation is a form of oppression that afflicts, embitters, and renders evil? It is a striving and longing that lead to contention between your flesh and your spirit. Vexation tosses you to and fro as your emotions fluctuate from highs to lows. Fretting, worry, and anxiety are agents of vexation, while their general is the spirit of insanity. They imprison you inside of a cycle of memories, thoughts, and regrets until you are disconnected from the present world. Vexation perverts one of the truths that I desire for all of you to be in this world, but not of this world. When you are vexed, it isolates you from truth, light, and reality. You are here physically, but your mind is not. Do you see the pattern?

Fret is a series of negative thoughts and emotions that consistently eat away at your peace. Entertaining every "if you had only," "you wish you never," or "you can't," agitates you into instability and inconsistency as you lose sight of who you are. It is a false teacher that causes you to depart from truth like Hymenaeus and Philetus (2 Timothy 2:17-19).

Recover your firm footing on 2 Timothy 2:15. Stop seeking the approval of man in your broken place. Study the solution through my scriptures instead of focusing on the problem. Walk through your broken place and refuse to stay in it. Persevere with diligence and hard work as I am the only one who can loosen shackles of vexation.

Think about the Gadarenes man. He probably fretted over what "they" said or did, how "they" seemed to be better off than him, or how he was like a beast before men and his God (Psalm 73:21-22). He lost all human connection as the vexation trapped him into an alternate reality. He was in the world, but not of the world while living among graves.

Then he met a man named Jesus who showed him a more excellent way. The man from Gadarenes found his delight in Him and wanted to follow Him in His ministry travels. See, beloved, the man from Gadarenes discovered a fivefold counterattack against vexation that comes from the first word of each verse in Psalm 37:1-8: trust, delight, commit, rest, and cease. Cease from fretting, worry, anxiety, frustration, and anger. Place your trust, delight, and commitment in me to receive my rest. Stop grabbing your cares in your hands like a toddler and cast them over to me. By employing these five words of strategic counterattack against the enemy's attack, you will receive grace and favor; they are spiritual fruit that you bear, and they define the biblical meaning of the number five.

Yes, daughter. I do see and care for you. You are fretting over the storm that has tossed you with winds and waves.

I hear the same trepidation of the disciples in your voice. They also asked Jesus, "Teacher, do You not care that we are about to die (Mark 8:38 AMP)?" He rebuked the wind and silenced the waves with three words, "Peace be still." The number three stands for the Trinity— God the Father, God the Son, and God the Holy Spirit. The winds and the waves obeyed His voice. The Holy Spirit is inside of you, daughter. The winds and waves of your life will obey your voice. Declare that same peace right now.

When will you focus on me instead of your broken place? How long will you mourn over it? When will you cease and desist from fretting and striving? Has this trial stirred up your doubt? Will you contend for a higher level of faith?

Love,
Abba

Where You Are

Dear Daughter of Zion,

Each of you has experienced a great loss. You feel like the wind has been knocked out of you. Job can relate. He lived a life that he thought was righteous. Job interceded for his children, yet he lost them, along with his possessions and health. Even his wife chided him to curse me and die. She found his breath strange and turned her back on him. Being in that place of brokenness and suffering confused him as he reflected on his past life and talked with his three friends (Job 13:14 AMP; Job 29:1-26 AMP).

His friends comforted him with their silent presence and solidarity for seven days. Then the magnitude of Job's loss captivated them into a dialogue of speeches about his righteousness. Job defended his innocence and pleaded for an opportunity to present his case. He didn't understand that his brokenness was not a punishment.

Walking upright before me never excludes anyone from suffering. I use suffering as a plumb line to test the strength of your walk. Job felt like he lost my glory. I only removed my hedge of protection so that my glory would shine that much brighter when I restored everything double (Job 42:10-15). Job's suffering allowed me to *demonstrate another level of my nature as I exposed a formidable enemy against walking uprightly: Leviathan, the king of pride. It takes a humble man to intercede for men who questioned the righteousness of his walk. Forgiveness, humility, and intercession were the keys to unlocking my manifold blessings in his life. As you process where you are, study the life of your spiritual brother, Job.*

Perhaps you are like Sarah, a living epistle written to me, who cried out for a season with heartfelt prayers as she tarried for the promise of a son. She became weary in the multitude of her own counsel. Frustrated with waiting for something that sounded impossible for her age, Sarah found a surrogate mother. When I sent my angels to remind Abraham of my promise, Sarah laughed in disbelief. After the angels heard her laughter, they confirmed the promise instead of rescinding it. Their confirmation reawakened her remnant of hope. It quickened her spirit to receive strength to conceive her seed, Isaac, the child of promise (Hebrews 11:11).

It hurts to hope when you wait for something and it doesn't happen. Among the witnesses who know human reason instead of divine moves, you invite unbelief and doubt into your life. Find comfort in Sarah. It took her twenty-five years before Isaac was born. Know that other women in the Bible received their sons from the dead (Hebrews 11:35). Among the witnesses of the widow from Nain, the widow of Zarephath, and the Shunammite woman, there are also others, such as Jairus, Elizabeth, Hannah, Samson's mother, and Rebekah who witnessed life springing forth from a dead child or a barren womb. They received what I promised them by faith, despite what it seemed like, and so will you if you have faith.

Perhaps you feel like Joseph. His future promise or dream did not match his current reality. He moved from pit to prison, unsure if he would ever graduate to the palace. Each place of transition led to promotion. The pit left him without natural resources, such as clothing, food, and shelter. Without the relationships he has always known, Joseph felt betrayed and abandoned. I was teaching him total dependence on me. Joseph relied on a coat to give him favor, but it was I who blessed the righteous and surrounded them with favor (Psalm 5:12).

Even in slavery and oppression, my favor opened doors. At Potiphar's house, Potiphar's wife tested Joseph's integrity and faithfulness through temptation. She told her husband that Joseph disrespected her, and Potiphar sent him to prison. What looked like a demotion was really an elevation. I caused the work of his hands to prosper (Genesis 39:21-23). Through my divine providence, I planned for him to be there so a baker and a butler could seek his gift of dream interpretation. The butler had been selected to be my mouthpiece that brought Joseph into Pharaoh's presence. Joseph's interpretation of Pharaoh's dream positioned him to be the second-in-command in Egypt.

When the famine led his brothers to Egypt and they realized their brother was alive, they bowed down and humbled themselves before him. Joseph's dreams had manifested into reality. He also gained the interpretation of his dreams. Not only did he reach a higher level in position, but Joseph also reached a higher level in spiritual growth. He personified my grace as he forgave his brothers. Joseph sought reconciliation instead of retaliation. The place of brokenness helps you gain a better understanding of what grace means, so you can exercise that same grace to everyone.

Brokenness, though painful, is my tool of spiritual development, and it has been a constant narrative in many lives within the scriptures. The woman with the issue of blood tried physicians of no value who couldn't properly diagnose the source of her illness. Broken in her health and finances, she touched the Source and was made whole. The woman with two mites functioned with barely enough for so long that she wondered if her little contribution mattered. The woman obeyed beyond sacrifice and still worshipped me through her giving. David lost three sons through death and family discord because of his transgressions. The issues of his heart flowed to me through his pen and his worship.

When I met the women in their health and financial crises, transformation transpired. When I stepped into David's broken places, healing and breakthrough happened. I'm waiting for you to invite me into your place of brokenness, so I can bring clarity to your confusion. You are so much like your siblings, Adam and Eve, your body poised to run and hide from me. I patiently pose the same question to you that I asked them: Where are you, daughter?

Love,
Abba

The Power of a Question

Dear Daughter of Zion,

I have been trying to talk to you. Hardship has made it difficult for you to listen; the burning in your heart lets me know you can finally hear me (Luke 24:32). I got you, daughter. I will never leave or forsake you. It is time for you to come into my classroom. Did you know that Genesis, the first book of the Bible, means origin? When you look at the beginning of something, you understand the connection between its starting place and its present place. Perhaps you have been asking yourself, "How did I get here?"

The enemy has kept you bound in smokescreens of shame, condemnation, and guilt. He has been distracting you from pursuing the purpose I originally desired for you. Adam and Eve had five words of purpose in the Garden of Eden: be fruitful, multiply, replenish, subdue, and have dominion (Genesis 1:28). The enemy used questions to create doubt, spark rebellion, and birth disobedience in Adam and Eve. He deceived them into eating fruit from the tree that I commanded them not to touch. His goal was to abort their purpose because he knew generations depended on Adam and Eve fulfilling their assignment. Now questions had disconnected them from me and their kingdom purpose.

Their act of disobedience cost them access to the Garden of Eden. As Adam worked the land with sweat on his brow from heavy labor, he often asked the same question: "How did I get here?" He saw the ripple effects of sin filter through his sons when Cain murdered Abel because I accepted Abel's offering and rejected his brother's offering. Adam buried Abel and lost Cain to a vagabond lifestyle. He asked again, "How did I get here?"

Adam felt like his place of brokenness would be permanent, but with every course correction that he obeyed, I always had a promise attached to it. In Genesis 3:15, I declared that the woman's seed would crush the head of the serpent while it would only strike the heel. Adam bore another son, Seth. Enoch, Methuselah, Noah, and Abraham, righteous men of faith, came from the genealogical line of Seth. The promise was not lost because Abraham would be the one to establish my covenant and set the plan of redemption into motion.

Your questions about what has happened have driven a wedge between us. There is fallow ground inside of you. Those questions have become endless genealogies that have ensnared you into a tangle of weeds. Let me till the fallow ground of your heart. My promise is if you seek first the kingdom of heaven and my righteousness, all things will be added to you. You must transition from this broken place so you can birth your purpose. Lives that I have assigned to you for ministry are waiting on you. For if the gospel of your deliverance is hidden, the lost will not be able to see it (2 Corinthians 4:3).

The power of a question leads to open doors or forces closed doors to remain open. A door is an entrance to a *place that can yield an adverse or positive effect. Let's look back at Cain for a moment. In Genesis 4:6-7 AMP, I asked Cain an important question as a key to discourage him from opening the door to sin. I said, "Why are you so angry? Why do you look annoyed?" My questions make you aware of your spiritual position. They are the warning signs that alert you to impending danger.*

For Cain, his anger would not allow him to hear and respond. So, I asked him another question that I followed with a warning. I said, "If you do well [believing Me and doing what is acceptable and pleasing to Me], will you not be accepted? And if you do not do well [but ignore My instruction], sin crouches at your door; its desire is for you [to overpower you], but you must master it (Genesis 4:7 AMP)." This question was one of redirection. When I mention the word "accepted," not only do I mean that I will receive Cain and welcome him back into right relationship with me, but I also refer to exalting him in rank and character and causing him to swell or expand. When you bring me the best of you—your time, sacrifice, treasure, talents, gifts, heart, and obedience—your first fruits, you show honor. Then I increase you in wisdom, stature, and honor. Obedience is better than any sacrifice. Cain's disobedience opened a door that led to him being a vagabond. A vagabond is one who wanders without being settled or stationary in one place, always on the move with no peace of mind. It can bring upon indecision and an unsettling in your soul that can affect your prosperity and health.

If you are unsettled, you can't financially prosper. A spirit of poverty attaches itself to you because you beg or scour for provision. The instability and wandering spill over in every area of your life. That feeling of coming undone at the seams could be an outward effect of fretting and vexation that open the door to a vagabond spirit.

Fretting can also come when you vacillate in your faith and seek other sources of guidance for assistance. The vagabond Jews strayed from the spirit of the Lord and relied on their own conjurations to exorcise evil spirits during the time of the early church in Acts 19:13-20. They connected with the sons of Sceva, a Jewish high priest using the name of Jesus without the power and authority because they thought the prestige of a name outweighed the power of faith in the name. Again, the power of a question opened a door to attack and torment. An evil spirit declared he knew Jesus and Paul, but who were they? Questions challenge the authenticity of your belief in your name, identity, and position in me. When you allow fretting and vexation to wear away the essence of your identity, it opens the door to unwanted access.

Cain refused to hear correction; he would've regained honor if he had listened (Proverbs 13:18; Proverbs 11:24). Not only by being generous in his giving as an act of worship, but his generosity in love and peace with his brother would've restored and strengthened their relationship. Instead, Cain was forever marked as a murderer because he chose the power of anger over the power of a question.

Remember how I always say that I am Alpha and Omega, the beginning and the end? Study the first mention and the last mention of a word in the Bible. It will give you a comprehensive understanding of it. I have said that questions are keys that can unlock a door with the type of answer you give. If you look up the word "door" in a concordance, you will notice that its first mention is in Genesis 4:7 and its last mention is in Revelation 3:20. In the second verse, it is not sin waiting at the door; it is Jesus. He wants to come into your heart so you may feast on the peace of His presence.

Return to me and rest so that you shall be saved. Renew your strength in quietness and confident trust. Be willing to hear me, submit, and obey. Let the Holy Spirit become your Master Teacher. His anointing abides in you to teach you all things. Settle here in your faith in me, in the love of Jesus Christ, and in the hope of the Holy Spirit.

No, this place of brokenness does not feel good. I know you want it to end. I have also assigned a purpose for your pain. It broke you to draw you closer to me while I make you whole, set you free, and embrace you as my beloved daughter. I am seeking your heart because I want a relationship with you-- all or nothing. Will you turn your heart back to the Father?

Love,
Abba

A Famine of My Word

Dear Daughter of Zion,

Daughter, who has had your ear? Whose counsel have you taken instead of mine? Who told you that you can't be restored? Who has declared your end when I am the only one who can kill the body and the spirit?

You have been in a famine. Yes, you have eaten, but you cannot get full. You have drunk much, but you still thirst. You have worked every day and earned money, but you still have little. It is not a natural hunger, thirst, or provision that has placed you in this desolate place. You have been in a famine of my word!

I have been there beside you as you followed your own path, pursued your own wisdom, and submitted to your own will. You listened to the voice of your heart as you justified your sin: The heart wants what the heart wants. I only wanted you, but you did not hearken to my voice. You were like your spiritual brothers and sisters of Israel. You hewed out your own cisterns that held no living water. They became counterfeit substitutes for the fountain of living waters that I can only provide.

When you listen to other voices, your spiritual hearing becomes dull. It opens the door for the deaf and dumb spirit to enter. This spirit paralyzes your spiritual tongue as it prevents you from speaking life. The man from the coasts of Decapolis wrestled with that same spirit. It made him deaf and impaired his speech. I commanded that spirit to open his ears and loose his tongue.

The deaf and dumb spirit is not alone. It is like its demonic brother, Legion. It is one of many. It has become a nation inside of your soul (Genesis 26:22-23). It binds you into a lukewarm knot of lethargy, rebellion, unbelief, depression, and doubt. You lose your confidence as you become halted in life. That is why you have been feeling stuck.

Daughter, their goal is to ensnare you into a spiritual stupor that disconnects you permanently from my presence. I didn't send Jesus to destroy a veil for the enemy to recreate it. I will allow nothing to separate you from me.

Beloved, I am standing at the door of your broken places that you are trying to gather up and hide from view. I am here to open your spiritual ears, so you can hear what I am saying to you. I am taking off the muzzle of grief, depression, hopelessness, and loss. I command your spiritual and natural tongues to be loosed.

Now open your mouth wide, and I, the Lord God, will fill it with worship and my word. Worship scatters the enemy that has been trying to scatter you. I told Israel, my firstborn daughter of Zion, that I would gather them from all nations where they had been disseminated by their foes. I am now gathering the scattered pieces of your soul. Bind the deaf and dumb spirit and loose the spirit of the fear of the Lord (Matthew 16:19).

Worship me and loose the testimony of Jesus (Revelation 19:10). Let the spirit of prophecy fill your mouth and intercept the plans of the enemy. The spirit of prophecy *proves to be too strong for any evil spirit or the flesh that opposes the work of the Holy Spirit. Worship is your weapon because it invites my presence and silences all flesh (Zechariah 2:13).*

Don't rehearse the words that confirm your current circumstances. Those words are untrue and pale in comparison to what I say. The lying tongue is only but for a moment, but my lip of truth is established (Proverbs 12:19). Speak words of faith, and then my words will replace your words, and my thoughts will replace your thoughts.

Come and learn of my humble spirit. Loose yourself from the fear of man, the yokes of the enemy, and the burdens of this world. Take up my yoke. It is one of ease and protection. Place my burden on your shoulders. It is light enough for me to carry. Learn of my voice. It is not one of condemnation. I do not mock or ridicule you.

It is time for your famine to end. Hunger and thirst for righteousness, and you will be continually filled. Daughter, whose voice will you choose?

Love,
Abba

A Divine Change of Clothes

Dear Daughter of Zion,

Can't you see my arms extended out to you? Look at the new garments that I hold in them:

Robes of righteousness and grace. Tunics of prayers and an ephod of worship. A coat of many colors and a mantle of favor. A scarf of mercy and a royal diadem... Every beautiful trinket you can think of.

You have fine linen that is dazzling, white, and clean waiting on you. This linen is like no other. It embodies personal integrity, pure motives, unshakeable fortitude, strong posture, clear insight, godly character, and a righteous mouth. Daughter, you are my bride, and the marriage table has been set (Revelation 19:7-9).

Be like your spiritual brother, blind Bartimaeus (Mark 10:46-52). Cast off your old garments of sin, people's words, and the world's judgment. Let not religion continue to constrict you with the traditions of the law when Christ has become the law to make you right with me (Romans 10:4 NLT). You are redeemed from the curse of the law, so walk in the faith of Jesus Christ as my beloved child (Galatians 3:13, 36). My grace redeems you from the curse of your sins.

Ask Manasseh. He was a king who turned the people to idolatry and did evil in my sight. I placed him in the hands of his enemies. He rent his clothes in repentance. I heard his cry and delivered him; he set things back in order.

Ask Ahab. He resisted Elijah and partnered with Jezebel to kill Naboth and take his vineyard. I sent a word to him like Jezebel sent to Elijah when I made a spectacle of her false gods: May the dogs that licked Naboth's blood also do the same to him (1Kings 21:19). Ahab rent his clothes in repentance and humbled himself to me (1 Kings 21:27-29). He stopped allowing Jezebel's voice to be an oracle of error. He cast his old garments and responded to the word of truth. Grace saved him.

Daughter, no one is too far gone for me to redeem. I open doors of hope in your valley of Achor. I am forever married to the backslider as Hosea remained in covenant with Gomer. His marriage was a prophetic demonstration of my faithful commitment to you.

Put on the heavenly garments that represent the spirit, truth, and love of my kingdom. The garment of love is one that supersedes any worldly standards of beauty. It is a love that does not hide flaws; it puts them on display for my glory.

You are my long-lost daughter whom I have waited to return to me. I wrote about you in Ezekiel 16:1-14. You are the one that I have desired to spread my skirt over and wash away the residue of your past with the power of the blood of Jesus Christ. You are the one that I am lifting out of the miry clay and declaring one word over you: Live! Exchange those ashes for the beauty of holiness. Anoint yourself with the oil of joy and gladness and remove that *black veil of mourning. Put on the garment of praise and shake off that spirit of heaviness (Isaiah 61:3).*

Rent your old garments in repentance and attune your ear to the divine frequency of my voice.

Love,
Abba

The Purpose for the Valley

Dear Daughter of Zion,

You are in a valley of dry bones, and it is a part of your restoration process (Ezekiel 37:1-14). The first stage is spiritual brokenness. I am revealing the state of your spiritual house to you. I am showing you how I use brokenness to make you whole. Then I will align your eyes with my eyes, your mouth with my mouth, and your hands to my hands (1 Kings 17:21-22). The Holy Spirit will enter you like fresh wind and revive you. It is a spiritual resuscitation designed to get you up from the bed of languishing and move forward.

The second stage of the process is spiritual restructuring. Wrong mindsets, faulty foundations, and limited perceptions of me are the sand on which you have built your house. Now the winds and rain have come, and you have experienced a great fall. I will move away this debris and build your spiritual temple again.

The third stage is the best part. It is when your spirit will awaken to your true kingdom identity. Once you complete the spiritual awakening stage, you are ready to learn how to fight the enemy. What a beautiful thing it is to be awakened, beloved.

It is when you become a mirror image of me. You will be in the Father, and the Father in you. Oh, the fellowship that made me translate Enoch into heaven, you and I will have that same bond. Before you think, say, or do anything, you will turn to me like the disciple John laying on my chest and asking if your thoughts, words, or actions will please me. My faithfulness will sustain you from generation to generation as I establish the truth of who you are in the earth.

The fourth stage is spiritual training. You will allow my voice to become your voice as you release prayers and worship. You will develop a battle plan that will counter the enemy's attacks. After that training, you will be my soldier as I strengthen you with the divine threefold cord of faith, hope, and love.

My love for you is so wide, deep, long, and high that I didn't give your fall the permission to destroy you. I couldn't let you perish, but I also couldn't stand back and let you continue this path. Now I am causing you to stand. I am sending my support and angelic host to help you as I rebuild your identity in Jesus Christ and restore your covenant relationship with me. I am connecting bone to bone and laying down the sinews, flesh, and skin like a master builder. Can't you hear the sound?

The thundering of my voice has set off a rattling in the spirit. Breath has become wind, and wind is now flowing into your new wineskin. I am forming you out of clay again like my beloved 1st Adam. I breathed life into him, and he became a living soul. His act of disobedience introduced death, judgment, and sin into you, but I, Jehovah, the maker of heaven and earth, the master builder, had another set of blueprints (Romans 5:19). I formed the 2nd Adam, Jesus Christ, whose coming and presence are woven into prophecies from Genesis to Revelation. His act of obedience as a sinless sacrifice caused grace to abound the more. He became a quickening spirit that is reviving you right now, daughter (1 Corinthians 15:45).

Whom the Son sets free is free indeed. I am making you to know the truth, and my truth—not the world's—will set you free. Be strong and courageous, and you will be able to endure the process.

Love,
Abba

The Process of Bearing Fruit

Dear Daughter of Zion,

Your trials and tribulations are bearing such a fruit of patience that will enable you to maintain your faith and joy as each trial comes. I build patience through seasons of great adversity, anguish, oppression, warfare, and persecution. It is the process in which I use in restoration. You learn of my patience—a quiet strength, resilience, and hinder-part resolve through any storm (Mark 4:38).

Patience brings experience. You can only know me through experience, not head knowledge. Head knowledge makes you think your way through something and miss the revelation found in spiritual growth.

Experience is building up a reservoir of hope that will not make you ashamed. See, beloved, when I am done, the love of Christ will be shed abroad inside your heart, and a light will shine through you and draw all men unto me. You must sometimes suffer long through challenges to bear the fruit of longsuffering. The fruit of the Holy Spirit is not easy to obtain; they require faith with works and the development of your moral character. Beloved, this process will be no quick fix and no easy exit.
When I am done, you will stand like the soldier and kingdom daughter I have always intended you to be. You will be a part of a great army, no longer trapped in

a grave, but equipped with the armor of God and a restored hope.

Since I only know the end date of this process, you will have people who will speak words of discouragement and ridicule your attempt to rebuild your life. You will even have moments of doubt about being restored. Guard your mouth and be quick to listen, slow to speak and slow to anger. It is not your business or theirs to understand what I am doing behind the scenes. I have started a great work in you before you entered your mother's womb, and I have every intention to complete it.

These letters are my modern-day almond tree rods that I am sharing with you like I did with my prophet (Jeremiah 1:11-12). Before I called Jeremiah to be a prophet, he was a priest. Since I was appointing him to a higher position, Jeremiah became fearful. Being a priest developed his ability to attend to the people's spiritual needs and bring them before me; now I needed him to communicate my covenant needs to them. Jeremiah gave me every excuse for why he could not be a prophet. I sent him the visions of the rod and the seething pot to comfort him.

Did you know the almond tree is known as the waker? It is the first one to bloom. I watch over it, just like my word, to make sure it bears fruit in its due season. I am always awake, beloved. I never sleep nor slumber. When the weight of the process is too much to bear, write back to me. I'm here—always listening, speaking, and comforting.

Love,
Abba

The Secret Place

Dear Daughter of Zion,

Come sit on this rock for a while. Listen, everything is not what it seems. I am a God of truth whose word does not return void. I know what I placed inside of you when you were only a thought. Don't you remember that the whole world was a thought in my mind, and I spoke it into existence? The Holy Spirit hovered over it, and I declared and decreed, "Let there be light." I am now speaking light into your situation.

Yes, the darkness has persisted. It has a potent strength that creates breaches or openings in which something or someone breaks forth as in birth (Genesis 38:29) or in vulnerable points of attack (Nehemiah 6:1). Some breaches are designed to kill, steal, and destroy. Darkness often comes in when there is a breach in a relationship or in the mind, body, or spirit (Proverbs 15:4). The hardest breaches to repair are the ones made by people who are the closest to you. Sometimes pride, idolatry, rebellion, unforgiveness, or some other sin forms the breach.

The breach doesn't only affect you and your relationships; it also separates us from each other

(Isaiah 30: 1-2, 26). Daughter, you have lost sight of who I am. No need for despair. I am the repairer of the breach and the restorer of the paths to dwell in (Isaiah 58:12). Quiet your fears, your emotions, your thoughts, and allow my voice to fill you with confidence and peace.

You are my most precious daughter. I created you, first by a thought, then with a spoken word. As I formed you in your mother's womb, my bowels were moved with compassion. Don't be alarmed. When I say bowels, I just mean the heart, beloved. I saw who you would become. I saw every dark period, for I orchestrated it to show my glory.

Life is a series of wombs that are dark, but provision is always made. As a growing fetus, you received nourishment every day and lacked no good thing. You stayed in that place until you no longer fit in there.

Your mother's womb could be viewed in two different ways: a secret place or a suppressed place. A secret place is where I hide you so you can grow and be prepared for the next stage. A suppressed place is where your desire for the familiar traps you into dysfunction, and you become stuck and stagnant.

The suppressed place is demonically designed for death; it desires to sift you like wheat. It wants your light to be a sign of conquest. The secret place is divinely designed for development; it desires to transform you into a city that cannot be hidden. It wants your light to glorify me in heaven. You are in a womb right now; it is the secret place. The enemy wants to bury you here; I want to birth you.

Not only are you in a spiritual womb, but I have also placed your purpose in the secret place. It has been there inside of you like a fetus growing from trimester to trimester. Your purpose is in the third trimester, and your broken place is one of labor and delivery. This part of your journey has been uncomfortable for a reason. Your purpose is experiencing labor pains. It cannot thrive in the current conditions of your mind, body, and spirit. Everything within and around you must divinely align so that your purpose is healthy and impactful. I am bringing your purpose to the moment of birth. I do not shut up the womb of what I desire to deliver (Isaiah 66:9). Your purpose has a global and an eternal outreach.

Who is that person sitting beside you? Why, it is my son, David. I am hiding him from trouble in the secret place, too. Notice how high his head lifts above his enemies. Oh, the sound of his praises and worship invites me to inhabit them. He often wrote psalms to me in times of distress. Each line spoke of worship, reverence, and relationship. The nature of David's talk, thankfulness, and transparency flowed through the psalms and displayed the humbleness of his spirit and the resolve of his faith.

A kingdom purpose with global and eternal outreach grew inside of him. I chose him to be the king who would serve as the shadow and earthly pattern of Jesus, the heavenly King to come (Colossians 2:17 AMP). The spirit of abortion opposed the seed of his purpose. This spirit is one of your purpose's most formidable enemies. Its strongman is the spirit of the antichrist; its henchmen are a diabolical hierarchy, and the spirit of murder is at its core. Any divine seed is set to be at enmity with anything that opposes it.

We already discussed about the woman's seed crushing the head of the serpent. In Revelation 12:2-5, the Dragon waited at the opening of the woman's womb to devour her seed. The world that you live in and the flesh that houses your spirit are at enmity with me. Your old man is constantly grabbing the heel of your new man like Jacob did Esau when the twin brothers made their entrance into this world (Genesis 25:24-26).

The spirit of abortion worked through King Saul and King Herod when they felt like David and Jesus respectively posed a threat to their thrones. It manifested through Pharaoh when he commanded the Hebrew midwives to kill Jewish male infants. His decree endangered the life of Moses, the Israelites' future deliverer.

As King Saul pursued him, David moved from wilderness to wilderness and from stronghold to stronghold. Away from his father and brothers. Always on the move. Always looking over his shoulder. Darkness persisted in David's life. The cave of Adullam was a womb of development for him. I divinely arranged for the distressed, the indebted, and the discontented to find him there. David became their leader. The cave was a training ground to prepare him for kingship.

David battled with discontentment, distress, and debt during his time on the run, but he also had a powerful testimony of my protection, provision, and power. This broken place developed David's resilience, faith, and strength. He did not faint in the day of adversity, so his strength was not small (Proverbs 24:10).

David did not faint because he expected to see my goodness in the land of the living, so his hope in me increased (Psalm 27:13). Even though the spirit of abortion surrounded David with intense warfare, he kept his mind on me. Writing led him into worship, and worship brought him into the secret place. That secret place is my presence.

Abide with us as you always remember that worship is your secret place.

*Love,
Abba*

Time to Transition

Dear Daughter of Zion,

It is time for you to transition to your next. You must divorce your past and marry your future. The spirit of this world has launched an attack on you because you are my beloved. For you wrestle not with flesh and blood, but against principalities, powers, rulers of the darkness of this world, and spiritual wickedness in high places. Whatever has led you to rock bottom is just a tool of spiritual warfare. It is a false reality that you are allowing to become your truth.

You are not alone. I am here with you, beloved. As you pass through the waters of trials and tribulations, I am there to help you receive strength to stand and grace to endure. When you walk through the fire, I appear as another person like the pre-incarnate Jesus who protected Meshach, Abednego, and Shadrach in the fiery furnace (Daniel 2:23-25). I am the omniscient, omnipotent, and omnipresent Lord God (Isaiah 43:1-3).
Yahweh, the Hebrew God of Israel, the Deliverer who heard the Israelites' cries from oppression, is with you. Jehovah, the self-existing One, the warrior who prevailed by drowning the Egyptians and their chariots, is with you. Jehovah Jireh, the God who provided Abraham with a ram in the bush and secured his possession of the enemy's gates, is with you.

Jehovah Nissi, the banner that gave Joshua the victory as Aaron and Hur held up Moses's weary arms in the battle, is with you. I am the God who moved upon the tops of the mulberry trees and defeated the Philistines for David (2 Samuel 5: 22-25) and destroyed the three nations who opposed King Jehoshaphat in 2 Chronicles 20.

I am the God of transition. Whenever I open the path for you to advance, the enemy plots to stop you. He desires for you to stay in your present condition, so he sends intimidation, oppression, fear, lack, infirmity—whatever weapon he can think of— to deter you.

When you make a move toward restoration and recovery, you offend the enemy. How dare you try to put the broken pieces of your life together? How dare you dream or hope again? How dare you resist temptation and submit to me in holiness and obedience? How dare you stop following the enemy's path of rebellion and restore your kingdom position?

The spirit of Sanballat and Tobiah and the spirit of Rabshakeh are two modes of opposition that the enemy uses when you are trying to rebuild in your broken place. Recovery, revival, rebuilding, and restoration are modes of transition and breakthrough that these spirits fight against in spiritual warfare.

Sanballat and Tobiah mocked and antagonized Nehemiah and the Jewish exiles for rebuilding Jerusalem. When Nehemiah encouraged them with hope, Sanballat ridiculed them. Nehemiah combatted that ridicule and hopelessness by declaring that they will arise and build and Sanballat would have no right, no portion, or no memorial in Jerusalem (Nehemiah 2:19-20). His opposition of threats would not prosper.

As Nehemiah and his people made progress with the gates, Sanballat and Tobiah oppose them again by asking a series of questions to discourage them. He asked how the Israelites expected to revive stones that had been burned to heaps of rubbish (Nehemiah 4:2). Through each distraction of slander, false prophecy, deception, and fear (Nehemiah 6:1-16), Nehemiah and his people maintained their mind to work and kept rebuilding through prayer (Nehemiah 4:4-6). Be like Nehemiah when the opposition comes to distract you during your transition. Declare that you are doing a great work, and you cannot come down from the wall (Nehemiah 6:3).

In 2 Kings 18 and Isaiah 36-37, Rabshakeh, an Assyrian cupbearer, derides King Hezekiah and Israel by stating that I was not able to deliver them and they should surrender. Hezekiah turned to me in prayer and supplication as he sought the prophetic word from Isaiah. Rabshakeh's blasphemy stirred up my righteous anger. I sent an angel of the Lord to smite the Assyrians (Isaiah 37:36-38). The spirit of Rabshakeh is one of witchcraft, intimidation, and rebellion. Its strongman is the spirit of the antichrist. It opposes anything to do with spiritual revival. King Hezekiah had just led the people through a revival of their worship and a restoration of fellowship with me. Daughter, what obstacle has risen against you?

With each stage of David's transition to kingship, the Philistines opposed him. When Samuel anointed him to be the next king of Israel, David fought his first battle with the Philistine's champion, Goliath. When the Philistines heard that he finally stepped into his position, they garrisoned around David. When I gave David the victory, the Philistines regrouped and surrounded him again. As you transition into your place of restoration and finally settle into your promised land, the enemy is still going to attack. Do not let the attacks instill fear. Remember that I am the Lord, the God of your transition.

Hear my voice, Zion. My voice is walking through the cool of the day toward you. It is quiet, still, and flowing like streams of water. Daughter, I am bringing strength to you now. I am blessing you with peace. The wilderness is shaken up. I am mightier than the flood. You shall live and not die to declare my works.

You are the apple of my eye and my darling. For you are altogether perfect; there is no flaw in you. Everything works together for your good, making it into a beautiful tapestry of grace, love, perseverance, mercy, and strength. I declared everything that I have made as good, and daughter, you are very good!

All my creation brings me such joy. My most anointed cherub was no exception. Yes, daughter, the enemy that you know as Satan was once called Lucifer. He was the son of the dawn whose rebellion transitioned him into an angel of deceptive light who fell like lightning from heaven (Isaiah 14:12-17, Ezekiel 28:12-19, Luke 10:18, & 2 Corinthians 11:14). I dressed him in the most beautiful jewels and gave him the most important job in the world: to lead all of heaven in worship. However, the creation let pride in, and the spirit of pride breached his spirit and his relationship with me. Since he could not be God, he decided to bring darkness and destruction in everything I created. He turned a third of my children against me and introduced darkness like a foreign agent into the divine design of earth, but he forgot one thing: I AM THAT I AM.

There is no other god before me. I am Alpha and Omega, the beginning and the end. I am Elohim, the Creator of heaven and earth. I am the King of kings and the Lord of lords. Heaven is my throne & the earth is my footstool (Isaiah 66:1). You are my sheep, and nothing can snatch you from my hands (John 10:27-28). Not even him.

He wants you to believe that everyone has abandoned you because you have fallen. The enemy fell like an angel of light and transitioned from things above to things beneath. Because he cannot return to his high position, the enemy wants you to believe that darkness and despair are your final position. Not so, my beloved daughter. Worship me in the beauty of holiness and watch me command light to enter your darkness.

I'm here waiting for you with a mighty outstretched arm, ready to bring you out.

Love,
Abba

For a Time Such as This

Dear Daughter of Zion,

My daughter, Esther, dealt with a life full of transitions. Her family was living among the Jewish exiles in Persia. This transition was one of dislocation, dispossession, and captivity. Jeremiah prophesied to them that they would have their own houses and land, but they were in someone else's kingdom and out of relational fellowship with me due to disobedience and idolatry (Jeremiah 29:4-14).

Having her parents die during her early teens, she was adopted by her cousin, Mordecai. Esther and her fellow Jewish exiles became orphans. Natural death separated Esther from her natural father; a spiritual breach in covenant separated my spiritual children away from me. Persia allowed them to worship me, but some of the Jewish exiles followed the many gods there.

To move from one day having your parents in your life to the next day having them die is an uneasy transition that results in an abysmal void. Hadassah, Esther's Jewish name, had Mordecai step in as a fatherly figure to fill that void. He reared her and counselled her in the Jewish customs and faith. What if he hadn't adopted her? What if she was truly all alone?

The orphan spirit is one of abandonment and rejection. It leads to mistrust and fear. This spirit loves running away to avoid being hurt or to refuse being rebuked. It causes you to run away from destiny, healthy relationships, and divine connections that I have assigned to help you.

The orphan spirit creates an identity shift or crisis. You forget who you are because your identity was so wrapped up in the people who left you. It convinces you that you must manipulate and think of yourself only or remain in isolation. It whispers lies that you are helpless and so broken beyond repair. It holds you in an arrested stage of development. The orphan spirit is one of immaturity. It results in the person being frozen in the time of abandonment like a little child.

The way to combat this spirit is through the spirit of adoption. My word says that you have received this spirit, which gives you the right to call me your Abba Father (Romans 8:15). The spirit of adoption, predestined according to the good pleasure of my will, transitions you from sons to heirs and then joint-heirs (Ephesians 1:5 & Romans 8:17).

As a child of God, you have my promise that you will always have the victory to overcome the world (1John 5:4). When you gave your life to Jesus and believed that he was my son whom I raised from the dead, you were saved and born again as my children. (1 John 5:1-5; John 3:16; Romans 10:9-10).

Learn about the spirit of adoption and the spirit of sonship. Declare and decree that you know who you are and whose you are. Declare and decree my *promises during this season of brokenness to let the devil know that He is overcome by the blood of the Lamb and the Holy Spirit that dwells inside of you! He cannot have you, for I have redeemed you, and you are mine (Isaiah 43:1).*

Daughter, names are important because they shape your identity and character. For instance, the Hebrew meaning of Hagar is flight. Tamar means palm tree, and Anjeanette means grace. Hadassah means myrtle tree. The myrtle tree emits a fragrant oil, and it is a symbol of righteousness that has had a significant presence throughout the Bible. Esther is a Persian name that means star. The meanings of the queen's Jewish and Persian names played a role in each stage of her transition. As each of you examine the meaning of your name, you will understand its connection to your journey. The most important name you have is child of God. That name is one of an overcomer, a king, and a priest that brings glory, honor, and majesty to my name!

As Mordecai worked in a key position in the Persian government, he functioned as a guide during Esther's pivotal transitions. Esther went from living in Mordecai's home to living in the king's harem. Then she moved to the king's palace as his wife. This transition required Esther to make a decision (Esther 4:13-14) regarding Haman's plan to kill Mordecai and all the Jews. Esther hid her Jewish heritage up until this point.

Her faith shone as a star as she released the fragrance of prayer and fasting on the behalf of her people. God gave her a strategy that overthrew Haman's plans and saved the Jews. The book of Esther shows how she survived brokenness and rose to position for the purpose of inspiring her people to fight for their victory. She transitioned from orphan to harem girl to queen to deliverer and change agent.

Where is your transition taking you?

Love,
Abba

Mastering the Art of the Shift

Dear Daughter of Zion,

Jesus transitioned from the Lamb to the Lion of Judah when He died for the atonement of your sins and restored you to right relationship with me (John 1:28; Isaiah 53:7; Revelation 5: 5-6). The genesis, or the beginning, of His transition originated in the Garden of Gethsemane. He cried out for the cup to be removed, but He realized that my will preceded His will. His transparency had exposed His humanity, but the present suffering did not compare to the glory that would be revealed (Romans 8:19).

The journey continued as Jesus experienced betrayal, physical abuse, ridicule, accusation, abandonment, rejection, and mockery. Daughter, please hear me right now. Jesus experienced every emotion that you feel in your brokenness. He knows about moving in the right timing of transition. Study His example through the Gospels as a manual of how to navigate transition and brokenness.

A shift occurred at Calvary. He died after asking for everyone's forgiveness and declaring it was finished. Jesus rose from the dead three days later. He proclaimed all power and authority had been given to Him. The journey came full circle when Jesus ascended to Heaven to sit back on the throne (Philippians 2:5-11).

This is also your journey, especially when you realize your true kingdom identity and understand how brokenness is a major factor in your development. There are three stages that form your identity. Each stage may have several steps to complete. These stages are genesis (beginning), transition (shift), and perfection or completion (full circle). The stages are recurrent throughout your earthly existence. They are like the stages associated with your salvation: justification, sanctification, and glorification.

Salvation is when unbelievers:

1) realize they have sinned, but have been redeemed through Christ (John 3:16)
2) believe God raised Jesus from the dead (Romans 10:9-10)
3) confess Jesus is Lord (Romans 10:9-10)

Justification is being declared righteous through Jesus' atoning sacrifice for your sins (Romans 5:1-11). His death and resurrection justify you to be in right standing with me. You now have grace, peace, joy, hope, and access through your faith. You are no longer my enemy because of your unrighteousness. Justification is a seal of approval like the one that products receive from their manufacturer. I, the Creator, have sealed you for eternity through the Holy Spirit (Ephesians 1:14). You are Godly approved, beloved! My love justifies you when you think your mistakes disqualify you. I love the unworthiness out of you.

Sanctification is to be set apart or separated from the world and made holy unto God. It is the continuing work of the Holy Spirit (1 Thessalonians 5:23). You work out your salvation daily with fear and trembling as you shine as a light in a crooked and perverse world (Philippians 2:12-13). The fear and trembling are not negative; they refer to constant awe of who I am. You possess your earthen vessel in honor and sanctification as you walk in holiness (1 Thessalonians 4:4). It is a process of allowing the Word to purify and realign you in order to be used as a servant and witness unto me.

Sanctification is like clay on the potter's wheel (Jeremiah 18:2-6). Each transition, whether smooth or difficult, is the tearing down of a familiar form that still hasn't reached the standard of divine perfection. It kneads the lumpy clay and forms a new pot. I am the potter and you are the clay (Isaiah 64:8). I never stop perfecting that which concerns my broken vessels. I only ask for a broken heart and a contrite spirit as your sacrifice of humility and submission (Psalm 51:17). The setbacks and the constant hits have not stopped you from getting back up. They only serve to sharpen the iron within you and remove the dross that covers your shine. Sanctification is the earthly dress rehearsal for the wedding set to take place in heaven.

Glorification is the ultimate perfection of believers that happens during Jesus' second coming (2 Corinthians 3:18). It is when you attain the mark of Jesus Christ, and you will be a true reflection of His glory with no sin, sickness, or pain. You have come full circle as you exchange your earthly vessel for your resurrection body.

This process of transition is like a car that has been T-boned. The mechanic deems it unsalvageable; the owner thinks otherwise. He saves the car from being destroyed and restores it. The owner constantly makes repairs, puts on new coats of paint, and smooths out the dents.

Some of the dents mark extensive damage, especially on the driver's side where the other car made impact and almost took him out. While he is driving, the owner often becomes cautious when other drivers pass by that injured side. It is like a gaping wound that seems to attract more harm. Sounds like the car has a breach like we discussed before, doesn't it?

There are times when the car breaks down, but he manages to get it running again. It is a lengthy process of restoring it to its former place as a working vehicle. Through time, the car doesn't look like what it used to be. It is completely restored and can now sustain a higher grade of gas in its tank. Its engine roars with such force. The car is meet for its owner's use again (2 Timothy 2:21).

Master the art of the shift. It is time for you to transition into the lion within you (Proverbs 28:1). You are still of use to me.

Love,
Abba

Coming Out From Among Them

Dear Daughter of Zion,

Exalt me, not the situation, crisis, wound, or person. I am all that you need. I am your protection and provision. Daughter, everything that tried to take you out will turn into a steppingstone to strengthen your faith in me. It is only to grow you and show my glory, not leave you in shame and pain.

I, the Lord, will make it good. Just like a mother does not forsake the child of her womb, I will always be with you. Your walls are continually before me. You are engraved in the palms of my hands. I am the Lord thy God. Trust in me. Try me to prove that I am a God of my word, but do not hide from me.

Submit to me, the One who is full of majesty, power, and dominion. Resist the devil, and he will flee. I have anointed Jesus Christ with power and authority to heal those oppressed by the devil. He is a defeated foe.

Come out from among them. Come out from the doubt, the disbelief, and the discouragement. Why do you keep picking up these dead things that have no weight or value? They are unclean things that I have commanded you not to touch. You are wheat destined to thrive in the field. Separate from the chaff so I can be your father and you can be my daughter.

Why do you worry about people's opinions and your problems when they have no life in them? They are false prophets who can do no harm. I am the way, the truth, and the life. No one and nothing have power over me. All power is in me. I defeated death. It has lost its sting. The grave has no victory. The earth is mine and the fullness thereof, and so are you, child of God.

Look over there. Do you see the bird standing still on the riverbank? It is still and in sync to the rhythm of the spirit surrounding it. Do you notice how as you are walking that it doesn't move? The bird is aware of your presence, but it remains in position. You could be a threat to this bird. Nevertheless, it knows that it must assume the position and remain there to stay in perfect peace. The bird has connected to the rhythm of heaven and refuses to let go.

Be like that bird, daughter.

Get in sync with the Holy Spirit. Belt out a song of worship unto me. Let it be a sweet incense that flows into my nostrils. When I see you worship, I stop everything and take a seat into your situation. Settle your mind, heart, and spirit. Shut out the world and its fears and become one with your Father in Heaven.

When fear comes in like desolation and destruction surges forth like a whirlwind, kneel and pray. When distress and anguish come upon you, bow your head in submission, hide under the shadow of my wings, and call out to me. Seek me while I can be found.

Love,
Abba

The Strange Woman of Fear

Dear Daughter of Zion,

Wisdom is standing at the entrance of your gates. She is crying out in the chief place of concourse, uttering her voice in the streets, and beckoning you to enter her house of seven pillars (Proverbs 1:21; Proverbs 9:1-6). She has always worked alongside me (Proverbs 8:30).

Attain her wise counsel and sound understanding. It is better than any riches. She is full of witty inventions. Turn at her reproof and receive the outpour of her prudence. Be knit as one with her as Jonathan was with David. She is part of the covenant relationship that I share with you. With wisdom, you are free from the fear of evil, failure, catastrophe, and anxiety. Hearken to her and you will dwell in safety.

Fear is like the strange woman. She feeds you with the bread of deceit. Her lies convince you that whatever you are facing is bigger than your faith. If you continue to listen to her, you will be cowering behind the weapons that I gave you to conquer your fear like King Saul and his army.

The bread of deceit will turn into gravel and keep you stagnant. You have so much word inside of you like deep water that needs to be drawn out into action plans of faith and strategy. Fear is a giant that has no power behind its roar. It is a Goliath who has no authority. Why do you let it taunt you, dear daughter? This fear is unhealthy for you. It breeds dread and terror while paralyzing your mind and faith. Fear doesn't come alone. It brings seven other spirits so that they can make your soul their home (Luke 11:24-26). The goal of fear is to start a new beginning that makes dysfunction comfortable to you.

I did not create you for dysfunction; I made you to function as an heir, a joint heir, a king, and a priest in this world. The strange woman of fear has seduced you with her invitation to come in, eat of her bread, and accept defeat (Proverbs 9:13-18). You are not the only one.

Another man of faith fell under the spell of the strange woman. Elijah had just experienced the greatest victory. He confronted more than 800 prophets of idols, and the fire of God consumed their false altars. Jezebel issued out a threat that sparked fear into him. Spirits of isolation, depression, and suicide terrified him. The strange woman of fear took his eyes off me.

Her tongue was a sharpened sword that dripped with an adder's poison. Her words were staves of corruption and foul decrees. She was no match for my name. Instead of uttering David's decree of advancing with the name of the Lord of hosts, Elijah hid in fear.

The fear of the Lord is one of reverence, awe, and respect. It is the beginning of knowledge and a banner of protection. The fear of the Lord is the blood of Jesus applied on the doorposts of your heart that make the spirit of death pass over you. It is a healthy fear that minimizes the threat and maximizes my throne. Operate in wisdom and do not put what scares you on an altar. You are justified by the grace of Jesus Christ. That simple truth makes you the just, and the just shall live and walk by faith, not in fear. Stand beside wisdom in front of my throne and rejoice!

This is not the time to draw the curtains and pull the covers over your head. Cast not away your confidence in which you will find a recompense of a reward (Hebrews 10:35-37). This is not the time to give up. Stand still in patience and remain in my will. This is not the time to draw back. The promise may tarry, but it will come in a little while. Oh beloved, just keep believing so that your soul may be saved. Salvation has equipped you with the greatest weapon. At the name of Jesus, every knee shall bow, and every tongue shall confess that He is Lord.

Fear, bow down to the name of Jesus.

Infirmity, bow down to the name of Jesus.

Anxiety, bow down to the name of Jesus.

Insecurity, bow down to the name of Jesus.

Regret, bow down to the name of Jesus.

Torment, bow down to the name of Jesus.

Fear of the unknown, fear of failure, fear of success, fear of man, fear of not having enough, and fear of being alone, bow down because Jesus is Lord.

Talk back to the strange woman of fear with the words of Lady Wisdom.

Daughter, fear is not the only strange woman because she has split personalities. She can be fear, wrath, witchcraft, adultery, or foolishness. These personalities are works of the flesh or anything that causes you to do something opposite to what I have commanded you to do. The strange woman is a doppelganger and a counterfeit of Lady Wisdom. She is at the beginning of works that are not of God and birthed in flesh. Beware of where you choose to enter and set your habitation: Lady Wisdom's house or the Foolish Woman's house. (Proverbs 9:1-18).

The warfare begins in fear, but ends in guidance, faith, and reassurance through wisdom. I covered Elijah with the wings of my love as I led him out of the cave and into his purpose again. Now I am doing the same thing for you.

Love,
Abba

The Source of Your Life

Dear Daughter of Zion,

I am your abundant supply. I am the source. I can open doors you know nothing of, but I require you to trust me and be obedient. Decrease your thoughts and desires and let the Holy Spirit increase as you follow me.

Allow your life to be filled with the abundance that Jesus died to give you. Disconnect from hindrances that harden your heart, or you may not like what is revealed when my face reflects yours.

My son, King Solomon, shared his wisdom about your life being a mirror that reflects the state of your heart; out of your heart, the issues of life flow (Proverbs 4:23). When your countenance is aligned with mine, I shall be like water unto you, a place where your questions meet my answer (Proverbs 27:19).

Don't make scarceness your lot. I will not suffer your clothes to wear out, your feet to swell, or your spirit to thirst. Live by every word that proceeds from my mouth (Deuteronomy 8:2-4). I am bringing you into a land where you will eat bread without scarceness. Your whole being will be nourished as you will not lack anything. Sever your soul ties from the past and do not revisit it, or you will become a pillar of salt like Lot's wife—a monument to the old man who should have evolved into a new creature in Christ.

Do not choose the ways of your oppressors or envy them. Be an imitator of Christ. Today is the day for you to rise, take up your bed, and walk. Be loosed, daughter of Abraham, from every infirmity and burden. I did not create you to be bent down.

I see that you have noticed another name of affection I have given you.

In Luke 13:11-17, a woman suffered from an infirmity for eighteen years. It forced her to bend down and not be able to walk upright. Despite her condition, she faithfully attended worship services. Jesus came to the synagogue one day. He healed her, and she glorified God. Her deliverance angered the religious leaders because it occurred on the Sabbath.

Jesus had the perfect response to their objections. He said if they would lead livestock to get water on the Sabbath, then why shouldn't a daughter of Abraham be loosed from the enemy's oppression?

My son, Abraham, is the father of faith, the promise, the covenant, and the future generations of believers. His descendants would enjoy blessings and freedom because they obeyed my commandments. I promised him that I would bless those who blessed him and curse those who cursed him (Genesis 12:1-3). His descendants would have a great name, and in him, all nations would be blessed. The woman's condition went against the truth of my covenant. Abraham's generational blessings belonged to her.

Freedom, healing, and deliverance are my children's bread. You are a descendant of Abraham and a child of promise. Be whole. Be you. Regain possession of your bread.

Love,
Abba

The Right Position

Dear Daughter of Zion,

You are to stand erect like a soldier, armed and ready. Move forward through this rough terrain. Hide behind the trenches to receive the download of my battle plan. Advance on your enemy only when I tell you (Ecclesiastes 3:8). Why are you trembling?

You remind me of your brother, Moses. The enemy charged after him by force and with intimidation. My presence went before him like a cloud and behind him as a fire. At first, Moses was bold and confident as he encouraged the Israelites to stand still and see my salvation. I promised them that they would not see the Egyptians anymore. Moses and the people experienced protection and small victories as they got closer to the Red Sea. They reached their destination; a larger obstacle now stood in front of them.

Moses trembled, but I reassured him that I would fight for him as he went in peace. The waters became a wall, and he led them to their promised land. Moses was a general of faith, a leader, an intercessor, and a deliverer. Kind of reminds you of your Savior, doesn't he? Just like I encouraged Moses, now I am exhorting you in your time of need.

Anna is another one of my children who married young. After seven years of marriage, she became a widow. Those seven years with her earthly husband prepared her to be my bride. Anna mourned the death of her husband, but I didn't allow her to make her grief a permanent residence. She learned that no matter the circumstance, her maker was her husband.

I had a purpose for her to become a prophetess and an intercessor. She prayed, fasted, and prepared the way for the Messiah's birth. For 84 years, she faithfully served in the Temple day and night. When Mary brought Jesus, Anna rejoiced and ministered unto me. Do you see the common theme among these narratives?

Moses and Anna persevered through difficult life challenges. Anyone would have expected them to retreat to their beds and succumb to adversity. However, each person of faith drew close, worshipped, and prayed.

To be an effective soldier, you must understand the pattern of the heavenly host. Ezekiel entered an open vision of the heavenly host, my own spiritual army. The cherubim angels had two wings outstretched that touched each other. This connection symbolized a united front. They had the same mind, the same heart, and the same spirit. Their faces turned neither left nor right. They didn't break rank or lose focus. Wheels covered in eyes mirrored every move the cherubim made because the Holy Spirit was in the wheels.

There is no need to fear because the Holy Spirit is always with you. You are enlisted as a spiritual sentinel in my army. As I told Zechariah, it is not by might, nor by power, but it is only by the Holy Spirit that you can fight and gain the victory (Zechariah 4:6). The Holy Spirit forever makes intercessions on your behalf, along with Jesus Christ. Your prayers are sweet incense to the Holy Trinity. Tag team with us as you march forward to breakthrough and wholeness because together, we are the winning team. Daughter of Zion, my beloved soldier, get in position and pray your way through.

Love,
Abba

The Right Posture

Dear Daughter of Zion,

Forgiveness is important in your walk toward wholeness. You must learn how to forgive others and yourself. Look at Peter. He was in Jesus' inner circle as one of His closest friends. He saw Jesus in His transfigured form. I chose him to reveal Jesus Christ's identity through spiritual knowledge, not flesh and blood (Matthew 16:16-19).

Afterwards, Jesus proclaimed that Peter would be the rock upon which the Church would be built. Walking with Jesus gave Peter access, authority, and protection. He had keys to bind and loose. Peter could legislate in earth and heaven. The gates of hell could not prevail against him.

Daughter, you have this same access, authority, and protection. When you do not forgive, those kingdom functions are less effective. You think that you are punishing people by not releasing them from their obligation to you. You are imprisoning yourself in mental, emotional, and spiritual torment. Have you ever stopped to think that the pain in your body may come from unforgiveness and bitterness dividing the joints and marrow instead of my word (Hebrews 4:12)?

You are the Church now, and you, as a beloved child of mine, should be looking more like me when Jesus returns. Loving people where they are and loving yourself, flaws and all, are how unbelievers recognize you as my own.

Like you, Peter made mistakes. He denied Jesus three times and allowed his flesh to get the best of him when he cut off the soldier's ear. In his guilt, regret, and possibly self-condemnation, self-pity, and shame, Peter returned to what he knew. He went back inside the boat. It was a life that Jesus told him to abandon and follow Him. Peter felt like he didn't quite measure up to His standard.

But Jesus didn't give up on him. Before He ascended to heaven, He specifically asked for Peter to come with the other disciples to Galilee. In John 21, He greeted Peter on his boat, just like He did in Luke 5, to call him out of the lifestyle that I did not originally plan for him. With three repetitive questions, "Do you love me?" and one command repeated after Peter's response, "Feed my sheep," Jesus reminded Peter of who He was. He didn't beat him up and make him feel low by repeating everything he did wrong. So why are you beating yourself up?

Daughter, do you love me? Then let me show you what my plan and purposes are for your life.

Daughter, do you love me? Then forgive those who have wronged, hurt, used, or abandoned you, even those who refuse to forgive you.

Daughter, do you love me? Then stop punishing yourself for what you did or what you didn't do.

I've already forgiven the offense. I have separated it as far as the east is from the west. I have washed you with the water of my word and cleansed you with the blood of Jesus. It is time to forgive, fall back in love with me, and I will make the rough places smooth and the crooked places straight. I see your eyebrows have raised in confusion. What do I mean by falling back in love?

You have left your first love. When you choose to harbor unforgiveness in your heart, there is no room for me in it. You think that you are giving me your whole heart, but you are not. There are stony places that resist the planting of the word.

How can you love me whom you have not seen and not love your brother or sister whom you have seen? Loving those who reciprocate your love is how the world loves. I have commanded you to be in the world, but not of it. What if I never forgave you? What if Christ couldn't get past the offenses shown toward Him?

Beloved, repent for the unforgiveness. Do an about face, change your ways, and release it. Give me the deep hurt and live in peace. Unforgiveness and bitterness have manifested as a poison that has affected our covenant relationship. It has caused you to see me differently.

Crucify your unforgiveness that has become a stumbling block of offense. Let me renew a right spirit in you and purify your heart. Stop lying around the pool of Bethsaida. I am stepping into the midst of your constant rehearsal of the past. Do you want to be made whole?

If you are ready, then let's go.

Love,
Abba

The Misconception of Time

Dear Daughter of Zion,

It is time to reflect on the good things that have happened to you. Do not despise the small things. Think about small blessings that have occurred at the right place and the right time. What about things that you have often taken for granted?

Breathe in, breathe out. You are still alive, but are you really living or just existing? I have created you for more. I have equipped you with everything you need. I have given you talents, time, and treasure. The most important treasure is the Holy Spirit nestled inside of your earthen vessel. He is the main source of creativity, wisdom, understanding, knowledge, counsel, might, and reverential fear (Isaiah 11:2).

I only ask for you to manage your time, talents, and treasures as a good steward. Yes, time and treasure can be lost. If you are faithful with a little, I will make you abound with more. I can extend the time.

Ask my son, Joshua. As he fought a formidable foe in Gibeon, Joshua asked if I could make the sun stand still so he could get the victory. I granted his request. Ask my daughter, the widow of Nain who thought her son's time on earth had expired. I orchestrated a Kairos moment, an opportune time, for Jesus to cross her path and resurrect him. Time is in my hands.

No, beloved, your time has not passed. That is a lie that the enemy often tells you. That is why I caution you to not be ignorant of his devices. If you think that your time is gone, then you will not move forward, and you will remain bound. This device is known as despair or hopelessness.

My daughter, Naomi, wrestled personally with this one. Have you met her before, beloved? She was a beautiful woman whom I had blessed with a husband and two handsome sons. Her sons married Orpah & Ruth. When her husband and sons died, she abandoned all hope and fell in despair. Naomi changed her name to Mara, which meant bitterness, and pleaded with her daughters-in-law to return to their homelands. Orpah left, Ruth stayed, and providence advanced.

Naomi's soul focused on what she had lost and no longer could produce. She only knew of one way to continue her genealogical line. Despair had her thinking that I afflicted her by having her return home empty, but I had a plan already in place.

There is a time and season for everything that you go through. It unfolds before your eyes as the present. You don't know what will happen next, but it is not a surprise to me. There is a deeper motive or narrative that is at work behind the scenes, and it contains a blessing for you. That is why I ask you to trust me with your whole heart and lean not to your own understanding. Your understanding will have you missing out on your moment.

I had already chosen Ruth to be the great-grandmother of David, one of the key ancestors of the Messianic line. The suffering positioned Naomi and Ruth for their Kairos moment. Despite the enemy's lie, Naomi did have a kinsman-redeemer named Boaz. I used a barren situation to birth an industrious spirit in Ruth. She worked the field and her faith, found grace in Boaz's sight, and became his wife.

Daughter, do not view your brokenness as an inconvenience. Perhaps I have you here for such a time as this to position you to birth your destiny moves. Stop maintaining an account of your lost time, missed opportunities, and past mistakes. Be like the five wise virgins. Be watchful, prayerful, and ready with stored up oil. Keep records of the scriptures and the good deeds like the king did for Mordecai.

The Word contains seed that can yield a harvest of a thirty-fold, sixty-fold, or even a hundred-fold return in every area of your life. I have always given you seedtime and harvest. The Son is rising with healing in His wings. You are His little calf bursting from the stalls, strong and ready. The sickle is in your hand, and the harvest is ripe. It is time for you to reap the benefits of the word I have sown.

Love,
Abba

Timelessness Inside of You

Dear Daughter of Zion,

The flip side to this device of despair is thinking that you have all the time in the world to do something. Procrastination robs you of time. One of my wayward sons thought he had all the time in the world because he had so many riches. He even built up barns to store it all with no second thought of giving it to the beggar, Lazarus. So many opportune times were scheduled in his life for him to be a liberal giver and start a relationship with me. He ignored them. When it was time for him to die, he ended up in Hades.

The rich man saw Lazarus, safe and secure in Abraham's bosom. He asked Lazarus to dip some water on his parched tongue. I forbade him to do so. Abraham explained to the rich man how he had gotten to this place. He wanted to send Lazarus to evangelize his kinfolk so that they would escape his fate, but I knew they were just like him. Procrastination and greed had them deceived into believing that all in the world, including time, was theirs to waste and manipulate. Not even my prophets or a dead beggar would convince them otherwise.

Procrastination, like despair, is a poverty of the mind. It restricts you from viewing time the right way. It blocks thoughts of plenteousness and renewal. Daughter, I am the creator of time. I exist outside of time, for I am timelessness. I am Jehovah Olam, the Eternal God. I will always be your eternal refuge with everlasting arms strong enough to thrust out the enemy who desires to steal your time. It is not too late to plan and create the life you want to live. Ask me to guide you.

Timelessness is inside of you. It is there through the indwelling of the Holy Spirit. In the beginning, He was there with the Word, Jesus. They both worked beside me. The Word was light, and the darkness could not comprehend it. The Word became flesh and dwelled among the people. The Holy Spirit fell upon Jesus like a dove, and He sent that same Spirit to you as your helper and advocate after He ascended to heaven.

He knows my mind, moves according to my Word, and intercedes in prayers of groaning and murmurings that can be only understood by me. Together, we are the Godhead, and we dwell inside of you. When you love us, obey our commands, and spend time with us, we make our abode in you. We are always there when you abide in us, so you will never have to be bound by time.

You are an enigma to the man who operates by rational thought. To be completely honest, this principle of timelessness is one you are struggling with now. For how can this be, you repeat the words of Mary, mother of Joseph? You have twenty-four hours in one day, and a certain amount of years assigned to your life span. What does it mean that there is an eternity placed inside your heart (Ecclesiastes 3:11)? How can timelessness exist in a body that expires at a set time?

Daughter, you are a spiritual being in an earthly frame. I made you in my image, which means you have a trinity of spirit, body, and soul within you. Yes, your body has a set time of existence, but when you give your life to Jesus Christ, He has prepared a room for you. My house has many mansions. Those mansions are resurrection bodies waiting for your eternal spirit to inhabit. We are connected in a river of timelessness moving together like a stream of consciousness.

Where you end, I begin.

Love,
Abba

A Steward of My Word

Dear Daughter of Zion,

You are a stranger on this earth.

I have sent you on an assignment to spread the kingdom culture throughout the world like leaven permeating the dough. Dough is also unformed bread. It takes time for the yeast and heat to develop it. Before you give your life to Christ, you are unformed. That is why I sent the bread of heaven as a path to salvation. As my temple, you continuously fill yourself with the bread of my word. You are responsible for imparting that bread into someone else. Don't be selfish with the teachings and revelations you receive. They are deposited into you to distribute during divine appointments.

It is time for you to progress from the milk of my word (Hebrews 5:12). I am calling you to digest, discern, and disseminate the meat of my word. Before a person becomes a chef, she only knows food in a simple manner. It ends her hunger and pleases her taste buds. Then she moves from just eating her food to digesting her food. The woman takes her time to chew and figure out the different components of each item on her plate. Then she discerns the different flavors and how they work together to create each item. Finally, the woman plays around with the different ingredients to make her own signature dish to share with others.

You must digest the scriptures. Spend time on one verse by breaking down each word, studying the Greek and Latin meanings, and seeking the Holy Spirit for understanding. Meditate on it, write about it in your journal, and even teach or discuss it with someone. Become one with the Word, but not too familiar with it. Ask the Holy Spirit to give you new insight into scriptures you have studied before. Discern the revelations within the word and its applications in living. Then disseminate what you have learned by putting it into action, strategy, counsel, or evangelistic missions. The timing and timeliness of the received word are important to the spread of kingdom culture.

That is why David asked me not to hide the commandments from him. The Word is timeless; once spoken, it doesn't expire. It is not bound by time. Your failure to speak it, move in Issachar timing, and receive it is what causes the delay for manifestation.

Daughter, the world has convinced you that time is a construct that no one can control. It is black and white with no shades of gray. The carnal man speaks Murphy's Law, along with his own wisdom that's custom-tailored by information. I make the foolish things to confuse their wisdom, and the weak, base, and despised to confound their standard (1 Corinthians 1:27-29).

The religious man knows that the law of the Lord is wisdom, and he knows that time is of the essence. To him, it is a time to follow every jot and tittle of the law. Those who don't cross every 't' and dot every 'i' are not worthy of his time or attention. They have become a lost cause to him. He assumes that they are forever lost to me. Not so, beloved.

The religious man believes that time, like one's word, is bond, something that cannot be refuted or regained. Do not eat of his leaven, for it is the same foolish wisdom that the Pharisees operated in when I sent Jesus. Beloved, I am the redeemer of time.

Indeed, word becomes bond, a bondage that makes my word of none effect. Jesus warned the Pharisees, religious men not after my heart, of this. By using it as a system of checks and balances, they were too spiritually blind to recognize that the fullness of time had manifested.

The One who knew no time stepped into time to bring an opportune time of salvation, but the Pharisees had no time to take advantage of it. Don't miss my move by being bound by a time that has passed.

Timelessness is inside of you. Potential is inside of you. Restoration is inside of you. Hope and greatness are inside of you. No one is stopping you but you.

Daughter, if eyes haven't seen, ears haven't heard, nor has it entered your heart what I have planned for you, what makes you think that the enemy has the upper hand?

He isn't that deep. Only I am.

Love,
Abba

This Kind of Longsuffering

Dear Daughter of Zion,

This season of brokenness is a time for me to correct the misconceptions that you have about me. One of those misconceptions is the meaning of love. The world defines it in ways that vary drastically from my original meaning. It is more than a feeling based on conditions. Love is a part of who I am. I am love.

Real love is the Greek word, agape. It means brotherly love, benevolence, affection, sacrifice, and merciful compassion. Do you want to know what real love looks like? Come closer, and I will share a few examples with you. Have a seat in the cleft of this rock as Moses did when I showed him my glory. Get comfortable and listen closely as I sit beside you to tell my story.

There is nothing you can do to stop me from loving you. Many waters cannot quench my compassion. Yes, I know you have made mistakes, but I will not deafen my ear to your cries. I overlook your mistakes and choose to focus on the good in you. I have longed to gather you like a hen gathers her chicks under her wings, but you were unwilling. Nevertheless, I am there with you every step of the way. That's what real love is.

I will always protect you with my shield of favor and correct you like a loving father. I walk with you as an extra person in a fiery furnace and deliver you with no sign of you ever being there. I also chastise you through correction in which deliverance is delayed, but not denied. This delay teaches you a lesson and gives you time to grow up spiritually.

It is me protecting you from self-sabotage because the wicked is lying in wait for you. That is why I ask my children to consider my testimonies. My testimonies are my laws and commandments. David talks about them in Psalm 119. They are counsellors and sweet expressions of my love. Like you, my spiritual sons and daughters of Israel did not consider them in every situation, but I never withdrew my love. Let me share how I loved them through their mistakes.

My people honored me with their lips and not their hearts. Doubleminded and unstable in all their ways, they found themselves in a continuous cycle: following my commands in awe of my miracles, operating in disobedience, suffering from enemy warfare and setback, heeding instruction from a judge, deliverer, or prophet, rededicating themselves to me, and then reverting to pride and rebellion.

Their oppressive bondage in Egypt was to blame. Egypt's polytheistic culture exposed them to many gods, and they really didn't know me well. After crossing the Red Sea and wandering in the wilderness, I taught them who I was, how I can provide, what my commandments were, and how to worship and obey me.

The Israelites had a sincere desire to worship me, but they were still enslaved. Their bodies fled Egypt, but they left their minds behind. For four hundred years, all they had ever known was a polytheistic culture. The Israelites had to retrain their systems of thought. I had to teach them what being holy and set apart to one God meant. Unlike my children, I wanted forever with them, but they were not consistent in their obedience to me. Their love, and yours, is shown through a willingness to obey me. The Israelites controlled how much influence I had in their lives. They consistently had one foot in the covenant and the other one ready to exit.

The Israelites enjoyed a life of abundance. Unfortunately, obeying my commandments became a checklist to complete instead of a relationship to maintain:

Attend the Sabbath at the tabernacle. Check.

Go through the motions at the festivals. Check.

Bring a sacrifice for the Day of Atonement. Check.

Return to disobedience. Check.

My children reasoned among themselves that everything was good. They had one foot in my commandments and the other foot in idolatry. They didn't trust my protection but compromised being set apart as mine for the favor of their enemies with no fear of my consequences.

Unfortunately, they were deceived. My prophets issued warnings of retribution and called for repentance. The Israelites had ears that would not hear, eyes that could not see, and hearts that would not receive. Since they refused to receive my word, I dropped the hedge and gave the enemy access. I sent Assyria, Babylon, and others as a rod of my anger and a staff of my indignation. For seventy-two years, the Israelites lived under the oppression of their enemies. I had a set time to restore them unto me and rebuild Jerusalem.

Isaiah prophesied about those years of restoration. Jeremiah reassured them that I knew the plans that I had for them to have an expected end full of hope. He told them that they would still have their own houses, marry wives, bear children, grow gardens, and seek the peace of the land while in exile.

During this season of my judgment, pride and arrogance produced fruit in the hearts of their enemies. They foolishly believed that I had turned my back on my children, and they had free reign over them as their gods. I showed them my glory and strength. I promised my people that the burden would be taken from off their shoulders and the yoke removed from their necks. Their yokes would be destroyed by my anointing (Isaiah 10:27). I even reserved the key of the house of David for them to open doors that no man can shut and close doors that no man can open (Isaiah 22:22).

My correction was not unto destruction; I loved them too much to sentence them to an eternal death that would lead to indefinite separation from me. Like you, they were my chosen ones. The proof of my love is they truly did not receive what they deserved, nor did they stay under their enemies' oppression. I redeemed them because they were mine. The correction was to humble them, restore my covenant, and purify their hearts toward me. Their love had been fickle and self-seeking. They suffered for lack of knowledge. Not all Israelites disobeyed. A remnant, or a chosen few, consistently obeyed before the exile or repented while under my judgment.

My love is steadfast, immoveable, and incorruptible. It is a grace and mercy following for the rest of their lives kind of love. It is a "laying down my life" for a remnant kind of love. Daughter, you are my remnant. Little foxes have attached themselves to you so they can spoil your connection to my vine (Song of Solomon 2:15). The vine represents your relationship with me and the purpose I have inside of you. These little foxes seek to defile my *concept of love by destroying the fruit of the Holy Spirit. I want to bear the fruit of my grace, mercy, and love in you. I am the rose of Sharon, and the lily of the valley; sit under my shadow and taste the sweetness of my word (Song of Solomon 2:1,3). Identify those foxes and let them rush out of your life to return their holes. Jesus has been seeking a resting place in your heart (Matthew 8:20). Real love desires all to be saved, healed, and whole. Will you let me bind up your wounds and heal the broken places in your heart (Psalm 147:3)?*

Love,
Abba

This Kind of Sacrifice

Dear Daughter of Zion,

I knew in advance that I had to present a sacrifice without blemish to reconcile my children and end the need for the yearly sacrifices for their sins. I had to create a way for you to come to me. Four hundred years later, I decided to send the Messiah.

I humbled myself, stepped down from my throne, wrapped myself in flesh, and became obedient to death. I came to the earth as Jesus. He was the fulfillment of the prophecy in Isaiah 7:14 and Isaiah 8:8 Emmanuel, God with us. Real love keeps its word, beloved.

Jesus became the physical representation of love. As the suffering servant, he bore your griefs, carried your sorrows, and shouldered the chastisement of your peace. Each of the thirty-nine lashes released healing from every past, present, and future illness. I didn't restrict the healing to the body; I am a God of peace who sanctifies you wholly—spirit, soul, and body (1 Thessalonians 5:20).

Real love is one that is sound and whole. I wish for all my children to prosper. I am faithful to keep you blameless until Jesus returns. To be blameless does not mean perfection as the world means it. It means to be complete, nothing lacking. The fire of adversity purges the dross from you, my most precious jewel. The dross is anything that stops you from being obedient and in right relationship with me. It is like the Egyptian mindset that enslaved the Israelites. The forty years in the wilderness purged the dross from them, but some of them would not be able to enter the Promised Land. In Numbers 16, the earth swallowed up Korah and his followers because of their rebellion toward Moses and Aaron. In Numbers 11, the fire consumed the Israelites because of their complaints about my provision.

Daughter, what is the dross that you need to remove?

My love endures forever. I never abandon the works of my hand. I'll perfect those things that concern you: the wayward child, the one who abandoned you, the illness that lingers, the hurt from abuse, or the struggle with finances, grief, or addictions. Whatever those things are, let my love perfect them.

Whenever I seek out to perfect a pattern, the accuser of the brethren sets out to pervert it. The enemy is like Nebuchadnezzar and the Assyrian king, the enemies who oppressed the Israelites. He thinks he has dominion over you because he has set you up to fail. Daughter, love manifested on that cross and refused to come down until he destroyed all the works of the devil. Walk in the power of that love.

My love is a banner that I spread over you as a seal strong as death. It is a standard bearer lifted like an impenetrable military band that does not fail in the time of battle. My love is my right hand that covers you. My right hand is one of righteousness, justice, authority, sovereignty, protection, strength, and blessing. It is where Jesus sits in authority, far above principality in heavenly places. Your seat is to the right of him. The prince can no longer take your possessions or your inheritance by oppression. Decree from my throne, daughter. Let my love help you regain your seat.

Love,
Abba

This Kind of Love

Dear Daughter of Zion,

Do you truly believe that my love is real?

My love is the shed blood of Jesus Christ. It purifies your conscience from dead works so you may serve me. It makes your scarlet sins white as snow.

While the people mocked Jesus and waited for him to die, Jesus granted a prisoner a seat in paradise and arranged aftercare for his mother through his disciple, John. As blood filled his lungs, he prayed for their forgiveness and yours. A makeshift crown of thorns crucified a carnal mind, and he willingly bore the pain; hence, the mind of Christ would be available to all who willingly received it. Jesus died to self while a legion of angels stood at the edge of heaven waiting for his command. Real love is commending your spirit to your father and dying to save a people who may still choose to forsake covenant. I know that last sentence is a little difficult to grasp. How could someone die for a people who continued to sin?

My son, Jonah, had a hard time with it, too. Nineveh really rebelled against me as a nation. I had given them several opportunities to repent; they still went back to their disobedience. I sent Jonah to prophesy to them. He knew they would repent and probably return to their sins. Jonah disobeyed my direct order. He ran away from his assignment by getting on a boat. I troubled the seas with a tumultuous storm. Everyone prayed to his own god for answers to why the boat was in danger. Jonah rested peacefully in the boat's lower level. The people drew lots and asked him why he didn't pray to his God. Jonah explained what happened, and the people reluctantly threw him in the water.

The storm ceased, and a whale swallowed Jonah. For three days, Jonah cried out, then repented and offered a sacrifice of thanksgiving. I delivered him, and he carried out his assignment. Afterwards, he sulked in anger inside a booth. I sent a gourd to cover his head from the sun, and then I used a worm to eat it. Jonah sulked deeper in his anger, mourned the loss of the gourd, and asked for his death. The gourd reappeared, the worm ate it, and a vehement wind blew as the sun shone down on his head. Jonah reacted the same way as he did before. I asked him, just like I did Cain in Genesis 4:6, if he thought his anger was a good thing.

I told him that the way he felt about the gourd demonstrated my love for Nineveh. I mourned for their wayward ways, but I loved them more to save them each time they backslid. It is the same with you. It grieves my spirit to see you broken, but I love you too much to let you stay that way.

I am El Kanna. I am jealous over you. You are my bride whom I have espoused to the Bridegroom, Jesus Christ. Many have come into your heart and constructed soul ties that have corrupted the divine pattern of my love for you. These soul ties are relationships involving people who know love in part while preaching a gospel that falls in line with the world's standard. Jesus is true love. He speaks truth that doesn't lie but embraces the real you.

His prophecies do not fail, and his tongue of kindness does not cease.

When you were a child, your speech, thoughts, and understanding about love were immature. It is time to put away childish things and pick up love, the greatest one among faith and hope. Grow into the full stature of Christ as you put on this kind of love that enables you to live your life in the bond of unity.

Love,
Abba

This Kind of Covenant

Dear Daughter of Zion,

Be like my daughter, Leah. Set your heart on things that are above as you reassess the treasure within your heart. Redirect your praise to me instead of man. Leah had her heart set on the temporal when she married Jacob. I understood the nature of the heart. Remember I told Adam that it was not good for him to be alone without a help meet, but she should not take my place in his life. Let me explain what these words mean.

In Genesis 2, a help meet is a complete person who stands beside you and aligns his God-given purpose with yours while still pursuing relationship with me. Adam's purpose was to work the Garden of Eden; Eve joined him in his purpose as his help meet. Her purpose was to be the earthly mother to my chosen people. She had the womb to birth the nations; Adam had the seed to help create them. They still walked with me in daily fellowship.

You are to be a man's complement, not a missing part to fill a hole that should already be filled by me. The world counsels you to find a soulmate; I tell you to find a help meet. Notice the word 'meet.' He comes and joins you in agreement with the divine design inside you. He meets a whole you, a woman who cleaves to him in flesh, bone, and covenant.

The divine pattern of relationships is first founded on me remaining as the head of your life and first in your heart. I choose someone who is going to love you the way I love you. Jacob didn't love Leah like I did, but man manipulated this union under my divine master plan. Laban, her father and Jacob's uncle, treated Leah and her sister, Rachel, as bargaining chips for control and manipulation.

Jacob really loved Rachel and wanted her as his wife. He approached Laban according to the custom. Laban dealt with Jacob through deception. On his wedding night, Jacob thought he was consummating his marriage with Rachel, but Laban sent Leah instead. He forced Jacob to go through an unfair trial to marry Rachel. Leah was not as beautiful as her sister, so he treated her like he really didn't want her.

Did you know that Jacob's name meant "trickster?" I won't get into it now, but let's just say that Jacob's mom, Rebekah, taught him how to be deceitful toward his brother, Esau. The trickster got a taste of his own medicine. One of my angels wrestled him, dislocated his hip, and changed his name to Israel. Israel means a prince who has power with God and man and prevails. He was a prince, not a trickster. I loved him too much to let him live in a false identity. Leah was more than a mistreated bargaining chip. I had a greater destiny planned for her, too.

I opened her womb to birth six sons who would become fathers of six tribes of Israel. Rachel, her maidservant, Bilhah, and Leah's maidservant, ZIlpah, would each bear two sons who would father the other six tribes. The twelve tribes of Israel were a model of my kingdom government in earth. I fulfilled my promise to make Abraham a father of many nations.

I favored Leah by closing Rachel's womb; the sisters' wombs were never opened at the same time. For a while, Rachel thought she would be barren forever until she gave birth to Joseph. With each birth, Leah thought I was trying to make Jacob love her. Each response spoke of her being unwanted and unloved. It glorified self and situations. When she had Judah, she found her praise and renewed her reverence of me. She realized what real love is.

Daughter, my love never fails. Man's love may fail, but mine is everlasting. I don't love like you do. Fall in love with me like I have fallen in love with you. For you are my beloved, bone of my bone and flesh of my flesh. My covenant is the example of how love and relationships should be. Spend time with me in the Word, so you may fully know my love. For in my love is victory, wholeness, and breakthrough. I really do love everything about you.

This season will not take you out. I brought you out to get the glory. Only I can heal and deliver you. Do not accept your circumstances as your end, your identity, or your set place. I am the resurrection and the life. Jesus has crushed the enemy's head with his heel. Because of love, He died to become the seed that breaks the cycle. That cycle or situation that you are in is a Lazarus tomb. I am calling you out by your name. I do not break my covenant or alter the things I speak from my lips (Psalm 89:34).

This kind of covenant removes the sting of death and defies the grave's victory. This kind of covenant never leaves you as orphans. Bind your heart to mine as you embrace your acceptance in my beloved.

Love,
Abba

Exposing the Enemy's Roots

Dear Daughter of Zion,

You are developing strong, healthy roots as you grow into my tree of righteousness with leaves that heal and fruit that nourishes (Ezekiel 47:12). You are much stronger, but you are not quite done with the process. Healing and deliverance take time to manifest into complete wholeness. You progress through many levels as you grow in your spiritual walk. Your goal is to reach the mark of the high calling of Jesus Christ, and you do not fully apprehend that mark until His glory is revealed in you.

Becoming whole is moving forward from strength to strength, glory to glory, and faith to faith. When you fully complete your transition from brokenness to your next level in wholeness, your testimony of breakthrough will encourage others and draw them unto me. I desire more of my daughters to be set free, and this deliverance will bring upon more warfare. Now it is time for your spiritual training to begin.

In Acts 16, I sent Paul and Silas to Macedonia to do missionary work. Paul received a vision from a man in Macedonia pleading with him to come there. Paul changed his traveling agenda and had Silas to accompany him. They immediately found the river where the ministry of intercession took place. Paul and

Silas ministered to the people and baptized Lydia, a prosperous seller of purple who invited them to stay with her.

Paul and Silas carried out the commission. They found a remnant, a small group of people who worshipped me without a synagogue. In Acts 16:13, the Greek word for prayer means a place out in the open where Jews could worship. The people became a house of prayer! They had the faith for salvation; the people only needed to go through the act of baptism to demonstrate their faith. Lydia and her family became the first converts. Wasn't that amazing?

Macedonia was a Greek territory ruled by Romans who worshiped idol gods. They included human kings and mythical ones, especially the one at Putho (Greek name means "python") where an oracle resided. Among this idolatry, people of faith persisted in prayer. Now Paul preached the spoken word (logos), and the Holy Spirit opened Lydia's heart to the revelation of baptism (rhema). She and her family transitioned from living under the law to living by grace. Others would soon follow their lead.

Paul planted the seed of the Word, and it spread like leaven (Matthew 13:31-33). A kingdom parable now became a living demonstration. My word refused to be bound (2 Timothy 2: 9)! The rhema or revealed word became their lifestyle. I delivered them from an oppressive way of life. Prayer invited me into their lives to be a present help in a time of trouble.

The enemy was not pleased. Paul and Silas experienced spiritual warfare that led to their placement in prison. The spirit of divination worked through a young girl. This spirit vexed Paul as the young girl followed him and Silas. She proclaimed that they were men of God who could lead them to salvation. The proclamation was true, but the spirit knew no truth. Its lying tongue wanted to maintain its hierarchy of oppression by establishing itself as having all knowledge and power. The spirit of divination is a familiar spirit that is limited in its authority. The Holy Spirit is omniscient, omnipotent, and omnipresent. The Spirit of truth worked through Paul.

Paul knew that demons believed and trembled at the knowledge of who I am, but they do not receive me as their Lord (James 2:19). Paul cast the spirit out of the young girl (Acts 16:18-19). Her deliverance became an offense to the men who used her for their own material gain. Paul and Silas divinely interrupted their system of oppression, manipulation, witchcraft, idolatry, and control. They laid axe to the root of Macedonia's problem. Let's examine this root.

The adversary had his three main principalities working through them. The spirits of Jezebel (witchcraft), Python (poverty, lack, hopelessness, and spiritual stupor), and Leviathan (pride) formed a demonic hedge. The Greek word for "divination" is python. The Greek words for "vex" are kataponeo and ochleo. Kataponeo means to wear down, to afflict or oppress with evils, while ochleo means to disturb or oppress with evil spirits.

Before Paul delivered her, the girl probably vexed the people when they prayed in order to break their faith. The spirit of python thrives on poverty, prayerlessness, lack, and spiritual lethargy. The spirit of Leviathan and Jezebel worked through the men because they wanted to be the town's gods. Paul flipped the tables within their marketplace like Jesus did in the temple and set the captives free to worship me in peace. Paul did what I commissioned apostles to do: set things in divine order. He brought down altars that did not exalt me as God. Paul dismantled practices that bore no fruit of faith.
I have given you three tools that can lay axe to the spiritual roots that have risen against you. In Acts 16:18,

Paul used the first tool: the power of the name of Jesus Christ (Luke 10:17-19; Philippians 2:9-11; John 14:13-14; Romans 10:13). His name is above all other names because He brought an open shame to all principalities and powers and triumphed over them (Colossians 2:13). Lay hands on your places of affliction and proclaim the name of Jesus Christ. There is power in His name, beloved!

The second tool is the power of the blood of the Lamb. In Revelation 12:11, He overcame the enemy through His blood and the power of your testimony. Plead the blood over your places of affliction. Plead the blood over your mind, heart, and spirit. Only the blood can purify your conscience of dead works so that you may be of service to me (Hebrews 9:14).

The last tool is the power of the Word. In John 6:63, the words of Jesus are spirit and truth; they quicken the spirit because the flesh profits nothing. The truth sanctifies you. If the words are spirit and truth, then the scriptures are key components of your spiritual armor: the belt of truth, the sword of the Spirit, the shield of faith, the gospel of peace, the breastplate of righteousness, the helmet of salvation, and praying in the Spirit (Ephesians 6:10-18).

When you expose and dismantle roots, you stop further growth that could lead to a barrenness of faith. If the roots are not dismantled, then you as a believer will not be grounded deeply in your faith. That is why Jesus cursed the fig tree, overthrew the money changers' tables, and then taught the disciples how to move mountains and pray effectively (Mark 11:13-26). That is why I blocked Paul's original plans to go into another region and sent him to Macedonia. A more important rescue mission needed the message of the gospel.

It was time for a fresh wind of the word to revive the people. Review the state of your spiritual roots. It is time for a spiritual awakening, to take place in you.

Love,
Abba

Reviving Your Soul

Dear Daughter of Zion,

Each of these spirits have subordinates that work under them, and they are still active today. Their goal is to leave you so broken that you remain oppressed. Think about it. Whatever broke you has attempted to asphyxiate your spiritual lungs. What does it mean to asphyxiate? It means a loss of consciousness or death because something or someone is hindering your oxygen flow.
The hits you have experienced tried to kill, steal, and destroy your spiritual breath. Once the breathing stops, so does the throbbing of your pulse. You have felt the effects of the hit. You receive the word, and it seems like you are not filled. There is a leak in your spiritual vessel, beloved.

Meditation is an important practice and an effective tool to help repair this leak. Let your soul pant after me like a deer pants for water; let the deep emptiness of your broken place call out to the deep wells of my living water (Psalm 42:1-2, 7). Find a scripture. Sit in a quiet place or play worship music softly. Close your eyes, remove all thoughts, and breathe slowly in and out. Focus on each word of the verse and breathe in. Breathe out the opposite of each word. Create mental pictures of each word and center your attention on them. Do you feel what is happening? You are recalibrating your spirit and releasing the python's stronghold.

Meditating on the scriptures teaches you to lay down in the green pastures and engage in the still waters as I restore your soul (Psalm 23:2-3). I am the door that leads to eternal life. I protect and provide for you as the Good Shepherd. I give access to pastures in which you may freely come and go. I came in flesh to give you abundant life. In me, you find security (John10:9-10 AMP). In my word, you receive the rush of my wind. Ezekiel prophesied as I commanded to Israel's dry bones to hear the word of Lord so that the rush of the wind may revive life. Meditation is a key strategy against the Python.

Do you remember when Jesus told the parable of the sower? The weeds choked the seeds that fell among them. The seeds represented the word. Think about when you are choking on a piece of food. Your breathing is obstructed until you expel it from your throat or windpipe. That food is nourishment your body needs to function; the air is an invisible substance that you need to breathe. Without breath, you cannot survive.

You have been hearing the Word, but you have allowed distractions and a heart and love that is not totally committed to me to make you spiritually barren (Matthew13:22 TPT). The scriptures are spirit and life (John 6:63). When you allow distractions, a divided heart, or a love of money or ambition to uproot the sown word, you lose your spiritual breath. A divided heart is a hardened heart whose soil will not absorb water or nutrients.

Meditation is a spiritual irrigation system that softens the hardened soil so that it may be watered again with faith, love, and hope. The Python spirit has opened the door for other spirits to enter through hopelessness. Like in Luke 11:24-26, this spirit has taken down the vacancy sign and *moved in its roommates to begin a new cycle of oppression; fret not, there is hope! You will not succumb to a great fall. Paul and Silas meditated on the Word—Jesus Christ. The mental picture set off a chain reaction to deliverance. Meditate on the scriptures day and night so you may experience good success (Joshua 1:8) Daughter, I am about to unveil the next step in the battle plan to you.*

Love,
Abba

Picking Up Your Tools of Warfare

Dear Daughter of Zion,

Like a real python, the enemy suffocates and weakens you. His goal is to get your mind, which is intricately tied to your soul. Pride enters your soul because you do not want to let anyone in to help. Depression kicks in and takes away your ability to pray, read, and receive the word. You are living in a spiritual stupor. The spirit of witchcraft convinces you that your way is the only option. You make decisions based on your emotions instead of wisdom. You have now undergone a name change and an identity shift. Once the enemy has total control of your head, he has regained the authority Jesus died to give you. Your brokenness is a power play for your soul and your purpose on the earth.

As we continue to look at Acts 16, we find out that the men stripped Paul and Silas, beat them, and bound their hands and feet in chains. The prison became their place of brokenness. You have been stripped bare by the enemy in your broken place. He has used every weapon in his arsenal to lock you inside of physical, mental, emotional, spiritual or financial prisons.

However, I have given you a blueprint of an escape plan in Acts 16:26 AMP: At midnight Paul and Silas praised God, and then "suddenly there was a great earthquake, so [powerful] that the very foundations of the prison were shaken and at once all the doors were opened and everyone's chains were unfastened."

Your worship and praise are keys to your freedom. Daughter, one sound can rend the heavens. When you charge the atmosphere with the Word through your adoration of me, you invite me into your situation. When you let out an utterance, a moan, or a wail, the Holy Spirit can understand it and intercede for you (Romans 8:26-27).

This is not the time to be silent. In Philippians 4:4-8, Paul exhorts you to always rejoice, pray, make supplications, give thanks, choose Christ's peace, and think on godly things. Paul and Silas could have focused on their situation and retreated into silence, depression, and defeat. Instead, they opened their mouths and glorified me. Their worship brought them deliverance and saved one of the Roman soldiers from suicide. He and his family received salvation.

Your worship is a weapon and a refuge. Acts 16:26 is one scripture that unpacks a spiritual warfare strategy. It helps you navigate seasons of brokenness. The verse is a foundation built on my word. With every foundation, there is a purpose for its construction. It is in place to support the structure of something that is being built. Your season of brokenness has resulted in a deconstruction of many areas in your life. Your life is like a spiritual house. You must rebuild it on the right foundation. As Proverbs 24:3-4 advises, you use wisdom to build it, understanding to establish it, and knowledge to fill it with pleasant and precious spiritual riches. The right foundation is reading the scriptures daily. When you know the truth, it shall make you free and tear down the wrong foundations.

With that freedom, you break the chains by communing with me. Always set aside quiet time to hear my voice.

That quiet time is spent in the secret place. It is a safe space for you to pour out what is in your heart. You can ask me questions, reflect on what you read or just crawl up in my lap and release your burdens to me. Continue to write to me in letters, poems, journal entries, or whatever you like. By sharing what's inside of you, you expose the wounds and allow me to heal them (Psalm 62:8). Release it, daughter!

Open the prison doors through prayers, declarations, decrees and worship. When you pray the Word back to me, I watch over it to perform it. When you declare the Word, you encourage yourself with my promises despite what you see. When you decree a thing, you call on the Word to defend you in the courtroom of affliction. You speak the keys into the atmosphere that you need to open the door (Micah 2:13). Whenever you have those negative thoughts and emotions, you repeat those promises. You can also practice fasting as an additional tool with your prayers, declarations, and decrees.

Prayers, declarations, and decrees are vital tools in spiritual warfare. Warfare is a battle to complete a journey. It is a strategy to plot resistance at every point of breakthrough. Warfare exists as a complex network of systems that include two other branches. Warfare is an overall battle that targets all areas of a stronghold. Its prime area of attack is your mind, which houses your thought life.

Will-fare partners with it as a subordinate and sparks a battle of wills—your will against mine. You must engage in daily crucifying of your flesh, wants, and desires. It is a fight for submission and obedience to me. The other subordinate is word-fare. David prayed that the words of his mouth and the meditations of his heart be pleasing in my sight as his redeemer (Psalm19:14). He also asked me to set a guard over his mouth and keep watch over his lips (Psalm 141:3).

Your mouth is a gate that must be guarded from enemy attack. You cannot declare a promise out of your mouth, and then backtrack and decree the incriminating false evidence of your situation. My daughter, word-fare causes doublemindedness, and a double-minded person is unstable in all her ways (James 1:8). You must maintain the mind of Christ and only speak what you desire to see.

Worship is the spiritual cord that binds the prayers, declarations, and decrees. It surrounds you with the presence of the Holy Spirit and the vision of your breakthrough as the enemy surrounds you with his warfare. You must prophesy like David that even though a host encamps around you, you will remain confident (Psalm 27:3).

What a powerful and effective strategy to send the enemy fleeing seven ways: PRAY the Word, DECLARE the Word, DECREE the Word, and SING the Word back to me! Put me in remembrance of my word (Isaiah 43:26). This strategy will help you revive your heart and your relationship with me. Let me give you an example of how this strategy works. A daughter of mine read and meditated on 2 Samuel 5:20 in her time of brokenness. Then she used the strategy:

- *PRAY:*
  Father God, I praise You as Adonai, my sovereign Lord. There is none like You. Break through my enemies like the breaking of waters. Break through those barriers that prevent me from reaching my breakthrough. Be a sun and a shield around me. Your word says that You give grace and glory. Your word says that You withhold no good thing from those who walk uprightly before You. Father, I ask You to break through my depression. Break through my unbelief. Break

through my worry and anxiety. Break through with the water of Your word. For You are the Lord of the breakthrough. In Jesus' name, I pray. Amen.

- DECLARE:
  I declare that every wall in my life is breaking like the breaking of waters.
  I declare that no good thing will be withheld from me.
  I declare that the spirit of depression and unbelief are broken in Jesus' name.

- DECREE:
  I decree that the joy of the Lord is my strength.
  I decree that the God is a God of breakthrough.
  I decree that I have the victory because God has broken through my enemies like the breaking of waters.

- SING (her song to the Lord):
  Breaker, come forth
  Breaker, come forth
  Breaker, come forth
  Let the bound be set free

  Breaker, come forth
  Breaker, come forth
  Breaker, come forth
  Let the bound be set free

Daughter, can't you hear the clink of the chains hitting the floor in a beautiful song of freedom? You personalize the scripture so that it fits your situation. Decree and declare what you want to manifest in your life. Jesus tells His disciples in Matthew 16 that anything they bind on earth will be bound in heaven and anything they loose will be loosed in heaven. When you pray, bind and loose. Bind the problem; loose the solution. Heed the unction of the Holy Spirit and prophetically pray, declare, decree, and sing your breakthrough.

The song of the Lord is not one of skill or talent. It is one of your heart. It is you adjusting your prophetic sight to proclaim my truth to your situation. The song of the Lord is not only entrusted to the Levites, psalmists, or praise teams. I have exhorted you through several scriptures to sing psalms and hymns to each other and to sing unto me (Ephesians 5:16; Psalm 13;6; Psalm 30:4; Psalm 95:1; Psalm 98:1,4-5; Psalm 147:1.)

The last part of the Acts 16:26 strategy is to move forward with the encouragement of your testimony. In Revelation 12:11, John writes that you overcome the enemy by the blood of the Lamb and the word of your testimony. Jesus tells Peter in Luke 22:31-32 that after his faith has been converted through his season of brokenness, he will strengthen his brothers.

Your testimony will help others to see how God brought you out of a dark season. Don't just speak the testimony in casual conversations. Write the vision of your broken place, the testimony of deliverance, and the lessons of love, mercy, grace, and relationship. You will walk in love and be a follower of my divine pattern. The Bible is a story of the brokenness of man and the breach in our relationship and how I kept my promise of sending Jesus to demonstrate my love and restore our covenant relationship. Write the story of our love so others may experience the same fellowship with me. Be the living epistle of Jesus Christ! (2 Corinthians 3:2-6).

Love,
Abba

APPENDIX

A FATHER'S FINAL CALL TO ACTION

Have you just experienced a setback? RISE UP!

For a just man falleth seven times, and riseth up again: but the wicked shall fall into mischief.
Proverbs 24:16

Do you feel the weight of the world on you today? RISE UP!

For whatsoever is born of God overcometh the world: and this is the victory that overcometh the world, even our faith.
1 John 5:4

Do you feel like you are stuck and are not moving forward? RISE UP!

But the Lord was with Joseph,
and shewed him mercy,
and gave him favour in the sight
of the keeper of the prison.
And the keeper of the prison
committed to Joseph's hand
all the prisoners that were in the prison;
and whatsoever they did there,
he was the doer of it.
The keeper of the prison
looked not to anything
that was under his hand;
because the Lord was with him,
and that which he did,
the Lord made it to prosper.
Genesis 39:21-23

Is life throwing out a hit or two? TAKE UP YOUR BED!

Arise, shine; for thy light is come,
and the glory of the Lord is risen upon thee.
Isaiah 60:1

*Are you ready to allow me to fill in every space
that you have been holding back? WALK!*

In light of all this,
here's what I want you to do.
While I'm locked up here,
a prisoner for the Master,
I want you to get out there
and walk—better yet, run!—
on the road God called you
to travel. I don't want any
of you sitting around
on your hands. I don't want
anyone strolling off,
down some path that goes
nowhere. And mark that you do
this with humility and discipline—
not in fits and starts, but steadily,
pouring yourselves out
for each other in acts of love,
alert at noticing differences
and quick at mending fences.
Ephesians 4:1-3 (THE MESSAGE)

A DAUGHTER'S PRAYER

Our Heavenly Father, who art in heaven, hallowed be Your holy name. Let Your kingdom come and Your will be done on earth as it is in heaven. I pray that You will bless every reader. May they hear Your voice and receive a special impartation of Your love, peace, light, and presence. Lord, please meet them wherever they are.

If they are entering a season of brokenness, I ask that You give them the reassurance that this broken place shall come to an end, and their expectation of faith shall be met. Remind them that You have a plan for them to give a future and a hope. Lord, let them stand on Your promise that what was meant for evil will turn for their good, and their testimonies will help save and inspire many lives.

If they are in the middle of a season of brokenness, give them the grace to stand, endure, and finish. Lord, let them write the vision and make it plain, believing that though it tarry, it will soon come to pass. As You draw closer to them, they will draw closer to You. Let them not be weary in well-doing. For in due season, they will reap what they sow if they faint not. Let patience have her perfect work in their lives. Let no weapon formed against them prosper. Lord, lift up a standard against the flood of the enemy and perfect that which concerns them. Be a sun and shield unto them as You give them grace and glory.

If they are coming out of their broken season, let their mouths be filled with praise! I pray for healing, breakthrough, and deliverance for your daughters. I declare and decree that every purpose, calling, and gift in them shall come forth, and they will be able to bring other sisters out through their God-given purposes and testimonies.

If any of Your daughters are not saved, I pray that they will come into the saving knowledge of Jesus Christ. Lord, let them learn who You are, who they are in Jesus Christ, and what Your purpose is for them. Silence the lying tongue of the enemy and let Your lip of truth be established. Let the eyes of their understanding be enlightened as they learn of the height, depth, width, and length of Your love.

If any of Your daughters strayed away from the faith, let me be a witness that You are always after Your prodigal children. Let me be a witness that there is truly nothing that can separate us from Your love. We may turn our backs on You, but You never stop loving us. Hallelujah! You wait patiently for the lost to come back home. Restoration is for my sisters. Lord God, You love each one of them. I pray that they receive Your unconditional love and get to know You again.

I pray the blessings of Numbers 6:24-27 over Your daughters. I plead the blood of Jesus over them. I pray that they will see the goodness of the Lord in the land of the living. In Jesus' name, I pray. Amen.

A DAUGHTER'S STRATEGIES

A plan (motive, wise counsel)
in the heart of a man
is like water in a deep well,
But a man of understanding
draws it out.
Proverbs 20:5 (AMP)

STRATEGY #1 FROM THE LETTERS: UNDERSTAND THE TIMELINE OF PROCESS

The Father's View	A Daughter's View	The Word's View
IN THE BEGINNING When the process of creating the heavens and the earth begins When the earth is in its broken state (void, no form, dark) Where you must see it first then speak it Where creativity purposefully edifies the broken pieces	ORIGIN Move from your former state It is where you are physically, emotionally, mentally, and spiritually It is your starting place	LET THERE BE Genesis 1:1 Declare what you want to see Maintain a set time of prayer to talk to God Rebuild through His wisdom, understanding, and knowledge *Pray and meditate on this verse: Ruth 1:22*
ABIDE Where you tarry for the promise How to endure How to persevere Where you remain	WILDERNESS Develop patience Respect God's timing Stop complaining or murmuring Learn importance of place, time, and condition	REST Ruth 2:8 John 15:4 Drink from the vine through daily study of the Word and worship Keep your mind focused on Him for perfect peace *Pray and meditate on this verse: Job 14:14*
AND IT CAME TO PASS Where God watches over His word to perform it Where His word does not return void	PROCESS It is referred to as the middle This is where weariness settles in Breakthrough is near if you hold on	NEVERTHELESS Luke 5:5 Be diligent and operate in excellence and faith. *Pray and meditate on these verses: Deuteronomy 28:1-14*

SUDDENLY	BREAKTHROUGH	NOW John 9:25
When the fullness of time comes When the miracle manifests	Witness the answer to prayers Move from broken to healed Set free from strongholds Deliverance takes place God displays His power to make impact at an opportune time	Praise God for the breakthrough *Pray and meditate on this verse: Ephesians 3:20*
DISPENSATION What God entrusts you to do as His children in the earth When you draw men unto Jesus by lifting Him up through your testimony	ACCOUNTABILITY OF REVELATION & TESTIMONY Put His Word into action for the next season of brokenness Release the knowledge of God's glory through your testimony Withhold nothing about God's goodness	BE A GOOD STEWARD Colossians 1:25 Share your testimony and revelations with others to edify, exhort, and comfort *Pray and meditate on this verse: 1 Corinthians 9:17*
ETERNITY When Christ returns When the Son of Man expects to find faith When glorification comes	NEW CREATURE Become like Christ so you can live forever with Him. Understand to suffer with Him is to reign with Him.	BE READY Matthew 24:42-44 Watch, pray, and contend for the faith *Pray and meditate on this verse: Revelation 14:12*

STRATEGY #2 FROM THE LETTERS: DEVELOP PRAYER TARGETS AND STRATEGY
(AN EXAMPLE TO MODEL)

Prayer Target: The Heart

Reflection	Relationship	Reproduction	Resilience
We must stand on the Word as our foundation. **Matthew 7:24**	We carry our cross daily. Our cross is to love up and out: love God, others, and ourselves. **Luke 10:27**	For anything to flourish, we must remove what is fruitless and prune what is fruitful so that it can bear more fruit. **John 15:1-5**	We must adopt the prayer warrior's stance and keep our focus on God. **Philippians 4:4-8**
<td colspan="4" align="center">PERSONAL APPLICATION</td>			
Study what the scriptures say about the heart. Write about the Word in your journal. Write letters to God. Process the Word through poetry. If people from the Bible are involved in your study of the heart, write letters to them or about them. Writing helps you process your discernment and connection to what you read.	Think about the current state of your heart. Think about the current state of your relationships: • With God, • With yourself, • With your spouse, • With your parents, • With your children, • With others. Reflect on how the state of these relationships may have affected your body, mind, spirit, and heart.	Remove the fruitless. Examine the source and cut it at the root. • What is not working in the relationship? • What is hindering you from bearing any spiritual fruit in your heart? Hone the fruitful. • How do you need to grow or move forward to the next level? • What practices or habits are working?	*Praise* His character *Prayer* His communication *Worship* His being Who He is *Word* His authority *Strategy* intercede with Him: • *Set aside* a devotional time. • *Incorporate* scriptures *you have studied* into your prayers. • *Ask the Holy Spirit* for wisdom, understanding, and redirection. • *Maintain* a spirit of expectation. • *Decree and declare* the verses daily. • *Praise* God in advance.

NOTES

NOTES

NOTES

ACKNOWLEDGEMENTS

To my Abba Father—

Thank you for giving me the grace and trusting me to be a vessel to write this book. Lord, thank you for having Your arms wide open to receive me as Your prodigal daughter.

Reader, what you hold in your hands is one of the many seeds God has placed in my spiritual womb and charged me to birth into this earth. It began in the war room at the 2015 Global United Fellowship Conference in Jacksonville, Florida. After receiving the prayer to receive the baptism of the Holy Spirit, the intercessor told me to go to the war room. Each area of the room had a prayer focus. As I sat in one of the areas and interceded for the prayer targets, the Lord gave me a vision and told me that everything that I went through would be used to help others through books, conferences, and other ministry initiatives. Those books would serve as the foundation of my kingdom purpose and ministry.

That same year, Prophetess Juanita Bynum came to my church. During her message, she shared her testimony. God had told her that everyone else had used her and He could use her, too. I wept so much because like Prophetess Bynum expressed in her testimony, I had also wanted a tattoo. I wanted a phoenix to cover my back because I kept being broken down to ashes, only to rise again. I never got my tattoo, though. I thought that I was no longer of any use to God. I was just happy to have a relationship with Him again.

When I served in the Healing and Recovery ministry at my church, I would send text messages of encouragement to the participants. That volunteer experience, Prophetess Bynum's testimony, and God's vision helped me to see that there was a purpose in my brokenness. He told me to take those text messages and write my first book for the ladies in the Healing & Recovery ministry. The book is not only for them, but for anyone who has been broken.

I have been broken many times in my life before 2012, but this type of brokenness had brought a godly sorrow that led to repentance, redirection, and reconciliation with the Lord. What broke me was not my end; it was the beginning of my purpose. Dear reader, there is a purpose in your brokenness, too. To God be the Glory!

Thanks to my parents, Willie and Vernita Alexander, Karen Diallo, Lakeisha Rogers-Rucker, and Nikki Robinson.

Thanks to my editor and book designer, Erica McGraw for helping me bring this book into manifestation with her encouragement and hard work.

To my daughter, Kamaryn—Thank you for being such an awesome, beautiful daughter! I am so proud of the young woman you are becoming. I know that you have such great talents and gifts inside of you that the world is waiting to see. You are going to be such a success. I know it has been hard to see me go through this season, but I hope you will see my resilience and faith to keep moving forward. Let this first published book be an inspiration to go after your dreams and God's purpose for your life. I love you!

To Minister Scott—Thank you for visiting me in the hospital when I had problems with being able to walk on my own. You ministered to me and gave me a bible. You read

Matthew 6:25-33 and encouraged me to not worry and trust God. I still have that bible and study those scriptures often. Matthew 6:33 is my anchor scripture. By praying with me and sharing the Word, you inspired me to begin studying my Bible again. God used you to lead me back to Him in 2012. If you hadn't ministered to me, I doubt that I would have started this path to re-establish a right relationship with God. May God bless you.

To my Bethel family—God, the Master Strategist, had assigned two earthly angels, Elder Karen Woodson and Pastor Zella Richardson, to guide me back to Him. They demonstrated the unconditional love, mercy, and grace of God when I first met them on December 4, 2013. These two women saw me in my most broken state, and they have seen the great work God has done in me. Little did I know that Elder Karen would train me in BMIT to be the teacher I would become and Pastor Zella would train me as an intercessor and embrace me as one of her spiritual daughters.

He divinely aligned my path to hear Bishop Rudolph McKissick, Jr. on Facebook. I see him as my spiritual father because his messages, transparency, and reverence for the Lord lifted up Jesus Christ and drew me closer to Him. During noon day services, gifted ministers taught me the Word and encouraged me. Soon, the hunger and thirst for God could not be filled. Watching Bishop McKissick, Jr. on Facebook was not enough. Listening to the sermons on Wednesdays at noon were not enough (even though I came home and rewrote my notes as a part of my study). Doing life with God my own way was not enough. God needed me to be all in with Him. He desired a covenantal relationship with me.

On February 3, 2014, I began attending Sunday services and Wednesday bible study. With each call to salvation, I felt the unction of the Holy Spirit to join, but I was afraid to commit. I had experienced church hurt. I had been rejected and abandoned. If I may be transparent, I really wondered if I gave my all to God: *would He break my heart and leave me like everyone else?*

I had a trust issue and a vision problem. I kept seeing God through the lens of religion instead of the lens of relationship. I equated the Creator with His creation. Bishop's sermon, "Death unto Satisfaction" was my wake-up call. I decided that I didn't want to die without completely reconciling my relationship to God. I could no longer be satisfied with where I was. It was time for me to put Him first. These divine appointments opened the door for me to rededicate my life to God on February 23, 2014. My anchor scripture for my life has now become Matthew 6:33.

Thank you, Bishop McKissick, Jr., Elder Karen Woodson, and Pastor Zella Richardson for the impact you have made in my life.

Thank you, Bishop McKissick, Sr., for your silent retreats that have taught me the practice of meditation and for your incomparable example of what it means to love unconditionally.

Thank you, Pastor Kimberly McKissick, for being a living example of how to submit to God's call to your life. Your journey has really encouraged me as I move forward in my purpose.

Thank you, Elder Darletha Lesesne, for your testimonies, your encouragement, your walk before God, and your prayers. You are another person who has helped me during a difficult season by reminding me of who I am in God.

Since joining, I've had several others in the body of Christ to speak life into me, sow seeds into me, and disciple me along my journey toward wholeness. I am grateful for them all.

To my mentor, Pastor Rosemary Winbush—I am truly thankful to God for divinely connecting me to you. I remember the first time that I met you at the SAGA women's ministry meeting. I asked you to pray for me. As I shared with you what was going on, you shed tears of compassion. This was the second time I had seen this type of sympathy. The first time had been when Elder Karen and Pastor Zella prayed for me. I expected judgment and condemnation, not compassion. You have such a big heart for people, especially for children. Thank you, Pastor Rosemary, for pulling out my potential, mentoring me, loving me, and encouraging me to embrace my prophetic identity. Giving me the opportunity to help lead BMIT restored my confidence to return to college-level teaching and pursue my spoken word poetry and old dreams again. You have always pushed me to operate in excellence and remember that ministry is about serving people and having a heart for them. Thank you.

To my readers—Thank you for taking the time to read this book. There is a writer in all of us. Writing creatively is not hard; it can be learned. Stay tuned for more strategies on how to write creatively and understand how the Word can help us in not only our brokenness, but also our daily lives.

FAITH | WORD | OPEN DOORS | CHANGE

www.ingramcontent.com/pod-product-compliance
Lightning Source LLC
LaVergne TN
LVHW051601070426
835507LV00021B/2700